THE MUSICAL JOURNEYS OF LOUIS SPOHR

THE MUSICAL JOURNEYS OF

LOUIS SPOHR

Translated and edited by
HENRY PLEASANTS

UNIVERSITY OF OKLAHOMA PRESS
NORMAN

By Henry Pleasants

The Agony of Modern Music (New York, 1955)
The Musical Journeys of Louis Spohr (trans. and ed.)
(Norman, 1961)

*The publication of this volume has been aided by a grant from
the* Ford Foundation.

Library of Congress Catalog Card Number: 61-9003

PREFACE

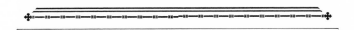

IT IS EASY TO FORGET that Louis Spohr was one of the great figures in the evolution of European music. Indeed, the musical world has largely forgotten it.

And yet, any lexicon will tell you who he was. Grove's *Dictionary of Music and Musicians*, in the third edition, gave him fourteen columns under his own name, four columns under "Symphony," one under "Violin-Playing" one under "Baton: Conducting," and a half-column each under "Opera" and "Oratorio."

He was certainly the greatest German violinist of his time (1784–1859), probably even the greatest of his generation, and his *Violin School*, completed in 1831, is still standard teaching material. Of his seventeen violin concertos Grove's article on "Violin-Playing" says: "They were, with the single exception of Beethoven's concerto, by far the most valuable contributions to the literature of the violin, as a solo instrument, hitherto made. Compared even with the best of Viotti's, Rode's, or Kreutzer's concertos they are not merely improvements, but in them the violin concerto itself is lifted into a higher sphere, and from being more or less a showpiece, rises to the dignity of a work of art, to be judged as much on its own merits as a musical composition as by its effectiveness as a solopiece."

Until his nine symphonies were eclipsed by those of Schubert and Brahms, they were held to be the best after Beethoven's. His operas, particularly *Jessonda* and *Faust*, enjoyed great popularity in Germany and England until overshadowed by those of Weber, Meyerbeer, Wagner, and Verdi. His major oratorios, *The Last Things, Calvary*, and *The Fall of Babylon*, preceded Mendelssohn's and rivaled them in popularity.

He was one of the very first conductors in the sense that we think of conductors today. Before his time, the director of an orchestra was usually the concertmaster, beating time with his bow when need be, and assisted by a pianist responsible for holding things together. Sometimes the man at the piano was also the director. Spohr was one of the first to recognize direction as a full-time job, and to recognize the efficacy of a roll of paper or a stick as an instrument for communicating the director's intentions in regard to rhythm, phrasing, and dynamics. He introduced the baton to England and, by example, encouraged its use on the Continent.

Spohr also wrote a book, and it is with this book, rather than with his musical works, that we shall be concerned. It is an autobiography, called in German *Die Selbstbiographie von Louis Spohr*, published by Georg H. Wigand of Kassel and Goettingen in 1860. An English translation was published by Longmans in London in 1865. I know nothing of this translation beyond Grove's reference to the *Selbstbiographie* as "a most amusing work deserving a better translation than it has yet found." A replica of the German original was published by Eugen Schmitz in the Baerenreiter-Verlag, Kassel and Basel, in 1954, a most welcome contribution, since the original is now very hard to come by.

My original intention was a new English translation of the autobiography, but a first reading sufficed to prove this impractical on two counts: (1) Spohr himself carried the work along only through 1838, and the remainder of his life was covered, rather lengthily, by his widow; (2) even the latter part of what Spohr himself wrote falls off in interest as of about 1822, when he settled for life in Kassel as musical director of the court of Hesse-Kassel.

After translating all of the Spohr original, it struck me as overloaded with material of little or no interest to the contemporary music lover. What had most excited my own interest and pleasure while translating was the account of Spohr's travels as a young virtuoso, composer, and conductor to Russia, Austria, Switzerland, Italy, England, Holland, Belgium, and France between 1800 and 1820, not forgetting his travels in Germany itself. Much of this account is quotation from diaries that he kept at the time. Mindful of the example of Burney's accounts of his journeys to Italy, France, and Germany half a century earlier and their usefulness to students ever since, I decided to forsake the autobiography as such and concentrate upon these journeys.

Certainly they offer an extraordinarily honest and instructive picture of musical life on the Continent at the
beginning of the fateful nineteenth century or, as one
might say, at the beginning of the modern era. It was a
time of transition, musically as well as sociologically. Musical dominance on the Continent had been shifting slowly
from Italy to Germany throughout the preceding century, and on Spohr's journeys we encounter Germans,
where formerly one would have met only Italians, moving
out to Russia, Italy, France, and England, bearing with
them the gospel of Mozart, Haydn, and Beethoven and
taking, as Spohr did, a patronizing view of indigenous
music and indigenous musicians wherever they went.
Henceforth Italy would be of musical consequence only
in the opera house, and even there not without evidence of
German influence.

It was also a time of paradoxes. Haydn was only recently dead. Beethoven was still alive, greatly admired
and even venerated, and we encounter mention of his
early quartets and sonatas in these pages as early as 1801
and 1802 in remote provinces on Spohr's journey to St.
Petersburg. But as famous and successful as Beethoven
was, or as popular as a Mozart or a Haydn, their music
did not dominate the public scene as it does today or even
as it did a century ago. It was the day of the virtuoso, and
the names that we encounter on Spohr's journeys are
those of Clementi, the Cramers, Moscheles, Herz, Field,
and Ries among the pianists, and of Rode, Kreutzer,
Paganini, Lafont, and Boucher among the violinists. They
were virtuosos all, and composers, too, for each of them
contributed to the exploration of the capabilities of com-

paratively new instruments, and each composed to accommodate his particular excellence. Among these Spohr, as a composer, doubtless stood out even more prominently than as a violinist.

Contemporary music was still fashionable, as it had always been in Europe and as it would continue to be for another century. Indeed, we find Spohr lamenting the neglect of older masterpieces in favor of contemporary trivialities. Consciousness of Europe's heritage of great music was to come later, and Spohr, with his reverence for Haydn, Mozart, and Beethoven, contributed to it. Such blessings are not unmixed. Even established masterpieces are competitive, since the public, once awakened to a formidable heritage, concentrates upon what it finds best and neglects that which is only very good or only sometimes excellent. Spohr himself, and Meyerbeer, and even Mendelssohn are examples of such neglect. They left much music still capable of providing a superior pleasure, but it is not quite so fine as Mozart's and Beethoven's and Brahms's, and it falls by the wayside. It is our loss.

Spohr's accomplishments as a writer of German prose hardly matched his accomplishments as a composer or violinist, but his writing was, at least, unpretentious, and in a time when complex sentence structure and a ponderous vocabulary were regarded as marks of excellence by the majority of German writers, he wrote with exemplary simplicity. This is in accord with and doubtless contributes to the picture we get of him as a man. He appears to have been a straightforward, honest, sturdy, conscientious fellow, the professional musician through and through, and disposed to regard his own work and that of others from the craftsman's rather than from the intellectual's point of view. This did not prevent him from demanding that his craft be treated with respect, and in the pages of his diaries we find him again and again insisting upon the musician's right to an honorable station in society. In this he followed in the footsteps of Mozart and Beethoven, particularly in his relationships with an aristocracy formerly accustomed to regard musicians as nomads or servants or both.

If he was conspicuously aware of himself as the representative of an honorable profession, he was equally aware of himself as a German, and in this awareness he reflected the emerging consciousness of nationality that was to play such an important role in Europe, not only in music but also in politics. He had much curiosity about the world beyond the Alps and the Rhine, as his travels prove, but what he saw and experienced was regularly exposed to comparison with German equivalents and found wanting. Of both the French and the English, we hear from him that they were "unmusical," and while he grants a certain musicality to the Italians, he disparages their musical practices, even their singing. This prejudicial attitude can become tiresome, but there is doubtless some justice in it too. The great Italian art which had nourished the budding German musical genius in the persons of Schuetz, Hasse, Handel, Gluck, Mozart, and, indirectly, Bach and Beethoven, was now looking to Germany for replenishment, while England, still dependent upon the Italians in the musical theater, was finding new pleasures in the instrumental music of the Germans and in that curious amalgam of Italian and German enthusiasms, the oratorio. It was to be a German century, and Spohr, as one of the first of the great romantic composers who gave the century its peculiarly German stamp, may be forgiven his awareness of German musical excellence and dynamism.

The task of annotating these journeys was lightened by the excellent work done by Schmitz for the new Baeren-reiter edition, although I have also consulted many other sources, particularly Grove's *Dictionary of Music and Musicians*. But like Schmitz, I have been able to find no record of certain of the individuals named. Where there is no note, the reader may assume that this was the case. In translating or not translating titles from German, Italian, or French, I have been guided by usage rather than consistency.

HENRY PLEASANTS

Bonn
January 26, 1961

INTRODUCTION

LOUIS SPOHR (although a German, he always seems to have preferred the French "Louis" to the German "Ludwig") was born in Braunschweig on April 5, 1784.

Both his parents were musical. His father, a country physician, played the flute. His mother excelled both as pianist and as singer. As a very young child, he sang duets with his mother in the family's musical evenings at home. Somewhere along the way, his father bought him a violin at a country fair. From that time on there was no doubt about his professional destiny.

There followed the familiar genius' story of instruction by provincial teachers whom he soon surpassed. His earliest public performances won him a neighborhood reputation. When he was fourteen, his father, a severe man, sent him off to Hamburg to seek his fortune as an itinerant musician. The trip was abortive. It was the wrong season of the year. The wealthy were summering on their

country estates, and there was no opportunity for concertizing. Having no financial reserves, the young Spohr
wisely decided to face parental wrath over the failure of
a mission, and returned to Braunschweig on foot.

If it had accomplished nothing else, the journey had
taught him the advantages of steady employment; and upon
his return to Braunschweig, Spohr sought and obtained
a position as violinist in the Court Orchestra of the Duke
of Braunschweig.[1] Spohr's description of his application
and audition throws an instructive light on the court customs of the time as they applied to the musical profession.
As this appointment led directly to the first of Spohr's
great musical journeys, it may be regarded as the beginning of that journey and the Spohr text, followed until
his return from St. Petersburg.

[1] Carl Wilhelm Ferdinand, Duke of Braunschweig, born 1735, ruled
from 1780 to 1806. As a youth he was a pupil on the violin of the local
concertmaster. Mozart's father, Leopold Mozart, said of him, "He plays
well enough to make a career of it."

CONTENTS

ILLUSTRATIONS

THE MUSICAL JOURNEYS OF LOUIS SPOHR

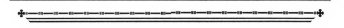

I

THE JOURNEY
TO ST. PETERSBURG

(1802–1803)

Upon my return to braunschweig, I addressed a petition to the Duke, describing my situation and concluding with a request for support in my further schooling or a position in his orchestra. Since I knew that it was the Duke's habit to take a walk in the palace garden every morning, I sought him out there with the petition in my pocket. Happily for me, he accepted it. After reading it hastily and making a number of inquiries about my parents and previous teachers, all of which I answered fearlessly, he asked me who had drafted the petition. "Who else but me?" I answered, almost offended by the implication of doubt as to my capabilities. The Duke smiled and said, "Well, come to the palace tomorrow morning at eleven, and we will discuss the matter further."

Who could have been happier than I! Punctually at eleven I presented myself to the attendant and demanded that I be announced to the Duke. "And who is this?" said the attendant, rather testily. "I am no 'this,' " I replied, indignantly. "The Duke has summoned me, and it is your business to announce me." The attendant proceeded to do so, and before I could recover from my agitation, I was shown in. My very first words to the Duke were, "Your Highness, your servant referred to me as 'this.' I cannot allow it!" The Duke laughed heartily and said, "Calm down. It won't happen again." After asking a number of questions, to which I gave the frankest answers, he said, "I have made inquiries about you with your former teacher, M. Maucourt,[1] and I am curious to hear you play one of your own compositions. This can be arranged at the Duchess' next concert. I shall so inform *Kapellmeister* Schwaneberger."[2]

Beside myself with joy, I left the palace and hurried home to prepare myself for the concert.

These court concerts took place once a week, and were thoroughly disliked by the orchestra, since, according to the custom of the time, cards were played during the music. In order that the card playing should not be disturbed, the Duchess had given orders that the orchestra should always play softly. The *Kapellmeister*, accordingly, employed neither trumpets nor kettledrums, and saw to it that the sound never reached a proper forte. As this was not always possible in the performance of symphonies no matter how softly the orchestra played, the Duchess had the players situated on a heavy rug in order

---

[1] Charles Louis Maucourt, French violinist, concertmaster of the Braunschweig Court Orchestra.

[2] Johann Gottfried Schwaneberger (1740–1804), for many years musical director at the Court of Braunschweig.

4

to further dampen the sound. Thus one heard, "I bid, I pass," etc., more loudly than the music.

On the evening of my first appearance, however, there were neither card tables nor rug. The orchestra, learning that the Duke would be present, had rehearsed appropriately, and the music went wonderfully. In those days I still played without a trace of self-consciousness, and since I well knew that my future depended upon my success of that evening, I played with true inspiration. I must have surpassed the Duke's expectations, for he repeatedly cried "bravo!" even during the playing. He came up to me afterwards, clapped me on the shoulder, and said, "The talent is there. I shall look out for you. Come to see me tomorrow." I hurried home, reported my success to my parents, and lay awake long into the morning, too happy and excited to sleep.

Next morning the Duke said to me, "There is a position open in the orchestra. You may have it. Be industrious and behave yourself. If, after a year or so, you have made good progress, I shall send you to some great master, for here you have no proper example." This last remark astonished me, for until now I had held the playing of my teacher, Maucourt, to represent the highest possible attainment.

Thus I began my fifteenth year as a court musician. The commission, made out later, is dated August 2, 1799. Although the salary was only 100 thalers, it sufficed, with thrift and the help of some extra work, and from now on I was no longer in any way dependent upon my parents. My professional activities included playing in the court concerts and in the court theater, for which a company of French singers and actors had just been engaged. Thus I learned to know French dramatic music before I learned the German, a fact not without influence upon the development of my musical tastes and upon my compositions of that period. Finally, however, for some special occasion, a German opera company from Magdeburg was engaged, and I was exposed to the beauty of Mozart's opera music. From that time onward and for the rest of my life, Mozart was my idol and my ideal. I still remember vividly the enchantment of the first time I heard *The Magic Flute* and *Don Giovanni*, and how I could not rest until I had borrowed the scores and burrowed into them, often far into the night.

Nor was I among the missing on other musical occasions, particularly since I joined all the quartet circles. In one of these, founded by two singers of the French opera who also played violin, I was introduced to the first quartets of Beethoven.[3] Thenceforward I was no less wrapped up in them than I had previously been in the quartets of Haydn and Mozart.

With such musical activity it was inevitable that both my playing and my taste should experience considerable improvement. I learned much, moreover, from two foreign violinists who visited Braunschweig at that time. These were Seidler[4] and the young Pixis.[5] The first im-

[3] Although Spohr does not give the precise date when he first became acquainted with these quartets, it was certainly prior to his departure for St. Petersburg in the spring of 1802. The six quartets of Opus 18 were composed in 1800 and published in 1801, and it seems noteworthy as an example of Beethoven's early popularity that they should have figured in house concerts in a provincial capital such as Braunschweig at such an early date.

[4] Ferdinand August Seidler (1778–1840), a well-known violinist of the time.

6

pressed me by his beautiful tone and his clear playing; the latter, by a technique extraordinary for his age.

I played often with the Pixis brothers at private houses, and publicly with the violinist in his second concert, joining with him in a double concerto of Pleyel.[6] After such stimulating experiences I returned to my studies with redoubled energy.

The Duke, who kept a fatherly eye on me, urged me to let him know whenever I played a new composition at a court concert, and sometimes appeared himself on such occasions, much to the displeasure of the Duchess, who was thus deprived of her card playing. One day, when the Duke was not present, and when, therefore, nobody paid any attention to the music, I tried out a new concerto of my own composition. More than a tryout it could not be called, since there were no rehearsals for these concerts, except on those occasions when it was known that the Duke planned to be present. Absorbed in my composition, which I was hearing with orchestra for the first time, I completely forgot about the rule against loud playing, and attacked the work with all the strength and fire of inspiration, carrying the orchestra with me. Suddenly a lackey tapped me on the shoulder and whispered,

[5] Friedrich Wilhelm Pixis (1786–1842) began his career as a child prodigy on the violin at the age of nine. After many years of concertizing throughout Europe, he settled down as conductor of the Prague Municipal Opera and professor of violin at the Conservatory in Prague. His younger brother, Johann Peter (1788–1874), was a pianist and toured with his brother before devoting himself to teaching in Munich, Vienna, Paris, and, finally, in Baden-Baden.

[6] Ignaz Joseph Pleyel (1757–1831), a prolific Viennese composer but more distinguished as the founder of the famous Paris piano-manufacturing firm of Pleyel and Company.

"The Duchess suggests that you take it a little more easily." Furious at this interruption, I went on, playing even louder. For this I received a reprimand from the court marshal.

The Duke, when I complained to him the next day, laughed heartily. But he also recalled his earlier promise and directed me to select a teacher from among the famous violinists of the time. Without hesitation I named Viotti.[7] This choice was approved by the Duke, and a letter was sent off to Viotti, who was living then in London. Unfortunately, he replied negatively, saying that he had become a wine dealer, occupied himself but seldom with music, and could therefore take no pupils.

Next to Viotti, the most famous violinist of the day was Ferdinand Eck[8] in Paris, and we turned accordingly to him. He, too, as it developed, was accepting no pupils. He had just married a rich baroness from Munich, where he had played in the Court Orchestra, and was now living the good life, partly in Paris, partly on the Baroness' estate near Nancy. He proposed his brother and pupil, Franz Eck,[9] as my teacher. The latter was then making a tour of Germany and had just enjoyed a resounding success in Berlin. A letter was addressed to him, inviting him, if he were interested in the proposal, to Braunschweig. He

[7] Giovanni Battista Viotti (1753–1824), one of the greatest violinists of his time and one of the foremost composers for that instrument, considered by many the founder of modern violin playing.

[8] Johann Friedrich Eck [not Ferdinand, as given by Spohr] (1766–1809), violinist of the Mannheim School.

[9] Franz Eck (1774–1804), brother of Johann Friedrich. Like his brother he played for a time in the Court Orchestra at Munich and, also like his brother, gave up his position, because of a love affair, to concertize.

8

EUROPE (1815–1914)

came, played at court, and made a favorable impression upon the Duke. As he was about to set off on a tour taking him as far as St. Petersburg, I was assigned to him as a pupil for a year's time, it being so arranged that I was to bear half the travel costs and that Eck, at the completion of the instruction period, should receive a suitable fee from the Duke. There is still in my possession a diary of this trip, some extracts from which may yet be of interest. It begins a few days before our departure on April 24, 1802. I was then eighteen.

Under the heading "Farewell," it begins as follows: "Among the saddest hours of one's life are those of leave-taking from loving parents and tried and true friends. They are assuaged not even by the prospect of agreeable and profitable travel; only time and the hope of reunion can heal such painful wounds. And it is to these that I look for relief as I set off on my musical voyage. So, farewell parents and friends! The memory of the happy hours of which you were the creators will always accompany me!"

We traveled first to Hamburg, where Eck planned to give some concerts. It was with a certain satisfaction and complacency that I now beheld again the city from which I had fled a few years before, so filled with despair.

After Eck had delivered his letters of introduction, we began our lessons. About this the diary contains the following, "Early today, April 30, Herr Eck gave me the first lesson. What a discouraging business! I, who considered myself one of the first virtuosos of Germany, could not play a single measure to his satisfaction. Rather I had to play every measure over at least ten times before he was even partially contented. He was especially displeased with my bowing, and I now realize myself that it must be changed. It will, of course, be difficult at first, but, convinced as I am that the change will be of great benefit, I hope to accomplish it."

The diary reports all sorts of things that we travelers heard and saw. But as attractive as all this inevitably was,

I permitted no diversions to interfere with my studies. The morning, which then lasted in Hamburg until three o'clock, was given over entirely to practicing the exercises Eck assigned to me. It wasn't long before he expressed his satisfaction with my progress. Under the date of May 10 the diary reports: "Herr Eck is beginning to be more pleased with my playing, and yesterday was gracious enough to assure me that I now play flawlessly the concerto I have prepared with him."

The periods between practicing I spent in painting. From my earliest childhood, I had drawn and worked with water colors and, with no instruction to speak of, had become quite good at it. Indeed, there was a time when I was undecided about which of the two arts to adopt as a profession. I now made my first attempt at portraiture. According to the diary, under date of May 12: "Sunday I began a miniature portrait, and finished it this morning. It is a self-portrait, and I am quite pleased with it. This and my practicing have kept me so busy these last four days that I have hardly left the house. I sent this portrait to my parents, and then began to paint Herr Eck, who has been kind enough to sit for me."

It is now time to mention that the young artist had always been exceedingly susceptible to feminine charms, and even as a boy had fallen in love with one pretty girl after another. It is, therefore, not surprising that the diary is frequently concerned with affairs of the heart. It is only odd how earnestly these passing affections are treated.

In Hamburg it was a certain Fraeulein Luetgens, daughter of a music teacher, who won my heart. After a visit to her father, I confided as follows to my diary: "His oldest daughter, a girl of thirteen, very pretty and innocent, pleased me immensely by her agreeable and modest deportment. She is very pretty, has naturally curly hair, fiery brown eyes and a blindingly white neck. Her father, whose passion was harmony and thorough bass, held forth on the combining and resolution of chords while I should have much preferred to hold forth to his daughter on the combining of hearts and lips."

In order to be near her more often, I asked permission to do a portrait of her, which was readily granted. But even before the first sittings I was warned by Eck, in whom I had confided, that she was a coquette and unworthy of my affections. At first I could not believe that a girl of thirteen could already be a coquette, but after the first sitting I began to share his opinion and reported as follows: "Henriette begged me to paint her in the dress she was wearing, assuring me that she had chosen it because her other dresses were not sufficiently low cut and covered up her neck. I was astonished by such vanity, and the sight of this charming neck, which would otherwise have delighted me, now disturbed me, for I was convinced that she was already infected with the vanity and shamelessness of the girls of Hamburg. While I painted, she talked with her cousin, a homely but vain girl, and about nothing but the dress she intended to wear to the ball the next night. . . . Thoroughly displeased, I returned home, hoping that we might soon continue our journey, as Hamburg is already getting on my nerves. My amiable heart, so open to all, will find no one here. . . . I thought that in this girl I had found one after my own heart, but I see that I have again been deceived. . . . I had thought to make a copy of her portrait for myself, but I am too bitter to do so. Nor do I have any wish to go to the ball."

But two days later I was writing "This morning I worked industriously on the portrait of Demoiselle Luetgens and also began work on a copy for myself. After lunch I went to her house. Henriette received me with reproaches for not having gone to the ball. . . . Today she was so modestly attired, and spoke so sensibly, that more time was spent in conversation than on the painting, as a result of which I didn't finish it. It is really too bad that this girl, with all her talent and good sense, should live in such a poor environment and thus be seduced by the follies of Hamburg."

With the presentation of the portrait and our departure from Hamburg soon afterwards, this romantic chapter came to a close.

In my comments upon what we heard in Hamburg, the diary gives its own ample commentary upon the state of my musical cultivation at the time and my views on art. These comments are, to be sure, given with all the naïve self-assurance of youth, and could certainly stand modification, if such were still possible after so long a time. The reports on operas and their performance can be dispensed with, since most of the operas have long since vanished from the repertoire and the names of those who sang in them forgotten. About some other accomplishments, however, including those of my teacher, the following excerpts may still be appropriate: "May 5. We were invited to lunch today by a Herr Kiekhoever, and there met Dussek[10] and several other musicians. This was a pleasant surprise, for I had long been anxious to hear Dussek play. Herr and Madame Kiekhoever are most pleasant people, and their home a nice combination of magnificence and good taste. Conversation at the table was in French, and since I speak French but little, I was unable to participate. The more eagerly, then, did I participate in the music which followed. Herr Eck began with a quartet of his own composition and delighted everyone. Dussek followed with some of his own piano sonatas, which were not particularly well received. Herr Eck then played a second quartet, which so delighted Dussek that he embraced him. In conclusion Dussek played a new quintet that he had just composed in Hamburg and which the company praised to high heaven. I could not wholly share their enthusiasm. Despite its many modulations, it became a bit dull. Worst of all, it had neither form nor rhythm, and the end could as well have been the beginning."

We remained in Hamburg until June 6. Dussek, who had charge of the arrangements for a concert on June 4, in connection with a festival staged by English residents of Hamburg in honor of their King, engaged Eck to play one of his violin concertos. Not until the rehearsal on June 5 did Eck discover that the concert was to take place

[10] Jan Ladislav Dussek (1760–1812), one of the earliest of the great piano virtuosos and composers for that instrument. He was for a time a pupil of C. P. E. Bach in Hamburg. He is also said to have been the first to place the piano sideways on the platform, thus giving the audience the profile view of the pianist that it has enjoyed (or not) ever since.

out-of-doors. A kind of canvas shell had been set up, in which the orchestra, some hundred strong, was placed in tiers. First Dussek rehearsed a cantata which he had composed especially for the occasion and which made a great impression upon me. Not only was it well written and splendidly prepared; but it also gained much through the use of a large organ which was situated behind the orchestra and which "sounding through the stillness of the night, had such an effect of solemnity that I was entirely carried away."

After the cantata, Eck was supposed to rehearse his concerto. But, concerned lest the moist night air have an adverse effect on the strings, and worried anyway about the effectiveness of the violin after such imposing vocal music and constrained between canvas walls, he decided not to play at all. In announcing this decision he also rebuked Dussek for not having told him in advance that the concert was to take place out-of-doors. This led to a stormy exchange and ended with our peremptory departure from the premises. Nor did we attend the concert!

We journeyed on to Ludwigslust where Eck had hoped to give a concert at court. Nothing came of this, nor were we any more successful at Strelitz, the court being absent. However, since the court was expected to return shortly, and since the friendly city, with its charming palace garden and adjacent lake, was most inviting, Eck decided to stay on there for the time being. As we had little prospect of better luck during the summer in Stettin, Danzig, and Koenigsberg, the decision seemed a wise one.

For my studies this was the most favorable period of our entire journey. Eck, with nothing else to do, devoted himself exclusively to the instruction of his pupil and initiated him into all the secrets of his virtuosity. I, in turn, driven by youthful ambition, was indefatigable. I rose early and practiced until sheer exhaustion compelled me to stop. But after a short rest I was at it again. Many days I practiced as much as ten hours, including the lesson periods. From Braunschweig I learned that some persons, ill-disposed toward me, were predicting no good outcome of my journey. They were saying, indeed, that I would distinguish myself no more than all the other young people whose studies the Duke had sponsored. I was determined to do my utmost to prove them wrong. When exhaustion threatened to dampen my ardor, the thought of my first appearance in Braunschweig upon my return would spur me on to new endeavor. Thus, in a short time, I gained such proficiency in the technic of my instrument that nothing in the violin literature of the time was too difficult for me. I was assisted in this by unfailing good health and a powerful physique.

I also found time to compose, paint, write, and read. Late in the afternoon we would go on outings in the surrounding countryside. One of our favorite pastimes was to cross the lake and have our supper at a little dairy on the opposite shore. I was already a very good swimmer, and on these boat journeys I would often strip and swim some distance alongside.

At this time I completed a violin concerto that I had begun in Hamburg and which was later published by Breitkopf and Haertel in Leipzig as my Opus 1. I also composed the three violin duets, later published by

Kuehnel in Leipzig as Opus 3. In practicing these duets with Eck, I discovered that my teacher, as was the case with so many violinists of the French school, was not a thoroughly rounded artist. As perfectly as he played his own compositions and some others that he had studied with his brother, he was unable to comprehend the spirit of foreign works. In these duets we actually exchanged roles, the pupil guiding the teacher in the manner of their performance. I also noticed, by an attempt he made at composition, that he could not possibly be the composer of the concertos and quartets that he gave out as his own. In later years the concertos appeared under the name of his brother, and the quartets under the name of *Kapellmeister* Danzi of Stuttgart.[11]

Thus passed four weeks, uneventfully but fruitfully, while we awaited the return of the court. One day, Eck complained of feeling ill, and had to go to a doctor. What passed between them remained a secret to me for some time, until the doctor finally decided to warn me that my teacher had contracted a disease in Paris and was now suffering from a recurrence. I still recall the horror with which I learned of this disease and its awful consequences, and it is probably thanks to this vivid impression that I have never been exposed to a similar danger.

Of my musical progress at this time the diary reports the following: "I can trace my improvement in no way more easily than by taking out old pieces from time to time and recalling how I used to play them. Today, for

[11] Franz Danzi (1763–1829), Musical Director in Munich, Stuttgart, and Karlsruhe and one of the teachers of Carl Maria von Weber.

instance, I took out the concerto that I had worked up in Hamburg and found that passages formerly very troublesome now went with the greatest ease."

Nor was my teacher wanting in encouragement. When I played my new concerto for him on August 16, he said, to my great pleasure, "If you continue to progress at this rate, you will return to Braunschweig a complete virtuoso."

Two days later, on August 18, I spent almost the whole day at home composing a new adagio for my concerto; for, although I had already written three of them, none of them seemed to go properly with the other movements.

As an example of my youthful artist's pride the following may be pertinent: "Everyone is talking about a folk festival to be held in Hohenzirze on August 27 to celebrate the birthday of the Crown Prince and to which the peasants from the surrounding villages are to be invited for dining and dancing. There will also be dancing at the palace. When I asked where the musicians would come from, I was told that the Janissary music[12] would play for the peasants, and that the Court Orchestra—imagine my astonishment!—would play for the dancing at the palace. I refused to believe it at first, but was assured it was so. But how was it, I asked, that the Duke could require such a thing, or that the musicians themselves could have so little pride and artistic integrity as to comply? The Duke, I was told, did not feel it unfitting that his orchestra should play for dancing, and the great

[12] A term used in those days to denote the percussion instruments in the orchestra such as bass drum, cymbals, and triangle. The term "Turkish music" was also used.

majority of the players did not dare oppose his wishes, since they were a pretty poor lot anyway and had little prospects of employment at other courts in case of dismissal."

We departed Strelitz on September 27, traveling by way of Stettin, and arrived in Danzig on October 2. As Eck had many letters of introduction to deliver and had also to arrange a concert, our lessons, which had hitherto proceeded with great regularity, rather fell by the wayside. I comforted myself with the thought that there was benefit for me just in hearing him practice.

Eck gave a concert on October 16 in the theater with great success. Since I was thoroughly familiar with the pieces he was to play, I took over their direction on the first violin. The musicians, who quickly recognized the security of the young conductor, followed willingly, thereby greatly easing the problems of the soloist, which he subsequently acknowledged. In addition to Eck's three numbers, the concert included a symphony by Haydn, an overture by Mozart, and arias by Mozart and Cimarosa. "The applause for Herr Eck was very enthusiastic and I thought it would never end. And, indeed, I have never heard him play better in public."

On October 20 in 1802, we continued on to Koenigsberg, where we remained until November 18. Eck gave two concerts, both well attended. But before he had given the first of these concerts, the Pixis family arrived in Koenigsberg on their return journey from St. Petersburg, and I was able to renew my acquaintance with them. The older brother had grown tremendously, and his soprano voice had become a deep bass. But he continued to play the child prodigy and dress accordingly. They were very dissatisfied with their trip to Russia, and the father claimed to have lost a thousand rubles on the enterprise, although he had arrived with two hundred letters of introduction.

We all met at a musicale given by Count Calnheim. It began with the younger brother playing some variations on the piano, which he did with brilliance and taste. Then the older played a quartet by Krommer.[13] Neither the composition nor its performance met with my approval. "His tone is weak, and his playing without expression. He has, moreover, such a bad bow technique that unless he changes it he will never become a first-class virtuoso. He holds the bow a hand's breadth from the bridge and raises the right arm much too high. Thus his bowing lacks strength, and the nuances between *piano* and *forte* are irrevocably lost." After him came Eck, also with a quartet by Krommer: "But heavens, what a difference. The contrasts between strong and weak in his playing, the clarity of the passages, the tasteful embellishments, with which he was able to enliven even the most insignificant compositions, lent to his playing an irresistible charm. And he was duly rewarded with unstinting applause. Pixis played a quartet by Tietz, the famous mad violinist of St. Petersburg, but had as little success with it as he had enjoyed with his initial effort. Finally he asked Herr Eck to join him in a duet by Viotti, in order that he might say that he had played with all the great violinists of his time; for Viotti, Rode,[14] Kreutzer,[15] Iwanovichi,[16] Tietz,[17] Du-

[13] Franz Krommer (1760–1831), a prolific composer of chamber music, the number of his string quartets alone running to some seventy.

[14] Jacques Pierre Joseph Rode (1774–1830), French violinist, pupil of Viotti, an outstanding virtuoso and composer.

rand[18] and others had already honored him in this manner. The entire assemblage seconded his entreaty, and Herr Eck had no choice but to comply. Pixis did his best playing in this duet, although there was not a single passage that he played as well as Herr Eck, who was utterly unprepared."

Not even in their public concert did the older Pixis win any applause. "The passage work was dull and without expression, there were many wrong notes and a deal of scratching. In my opinion he played better in Braunschweig three years ago when I first heard him in easy concertos by Iwanovichi than he plays in the more difficult things that he attempts now." Indeed, I doubted that he would ever become a great violinist, "unless he soon gets to a good teacher who will at least teach him something about bowing."

My teacher probably had much to do with these certainly too severe judgments, for he was a hard critic. When I heard Pixis ten years later in Vienna, he had grown into a fine violinist and served with distinction as professor of violin at the Prague Conservatory.

For the journey to Memel we chose the shore road, "which is twelve miles shorter than the inland road. Besides, in winter, when the sand is frozen, the going is

15 Rodolphe Kreutzer (1766–1831), famous French violinist and composer, to whom Beethoven dedicated the *Kreutzer Sonata*.

16 Iwanovichi, presumably Giovanni Giornovichi (1745–1804), a lesser virtuoso of the time.

17 August Ferdinand Tietz, born 1762 in Lower Austria, settled in St. Petersburg.

18 Presumably Auguste Frederic Durand, Polish violinist, pupil of Viotti. He specialized in technical tours de force and is said to have influenced Paganini's style.

easier. Three miles out of Koenigsberg one comes out right on the shore and stays with it the rest of the way to Memel. We traveled through the night and suffered terribly from the cold and snow-laden sea air. Between the fourth and fifth stations we had the misfortune to lose a wheel. We had to climb out of the carriage, pool our strength to right it, and fasten the wheel on with rope. This took a good half hour, and I feared that my fingers would freeze. They didn't. We arrived opposite Memel at nine o'clock, but had to wait a full three hours to be taken across the harbor, since the ferry personnel had to be gotten together from all over the city. Four miles further on we reached the border."

We continued on to Mitau. There, with the help of Eck's letters of introduction, we enjoyed the friendliest possible reception. We were invited out morning, noon, and night, to musicales, balls, and other festivities. On one of these occasions, I appeared for the first time publicly on the same program and in the presence of my teacher. As it happened, Eck, having played several quartets with great success, was urged to play a Beethoven sonata[19] with a young and highly accomplished sixteen-year-old girl pianist, but begged off on the grounds of fatigue. As I well knew that Eck would not dare to play something unfa-

[19] Presumably one of the three of Opus 12, published in 1799, although the Sonatas Opus 23 or Opus 24, published in 1801, are possibilities. Again it is noteworthy that these sonatas should have reached such a place so soon after publication. The Spohr original refers to Eck's having been invited "to accompany" the young lady, the piano at that time being considered as the accompanying instrument in a sonata for violin and piano. This concept of accompanying is carried even farther in Spohr's references to quartet playing. The first violin was the soloist and the other instruments played an "accompanying" role.

miliar at sight, I volunteered to substitute for him. The sonata was as new to me as it was to him, but I had great confidence in my sight reading. It went well, and I was rewarded with appropriate exclamations of approval.

After that I was regularly invited to play something at the various musicales to which we were invited. I well remember that a certain Herr von Berner, as we were taking our leave, said to me with fatherly benevolence, "My young friend, you are well on the way, just keep it up. Herr Eck is still superior to you as a virtuoso, but you are by far the better musician!"

At the house of the Governor I heard a violinist named Sogenoff, then very famous in Russia and a bondman of the Prince Surbow. "He played variations of his own composition, and of the utmost difficulty. The compositions I found quite good, but not so his playing. It was brilliant enough, but rough and offensive to the ear. Herr Eck played right after him, and the difference between the playing of the one and the other was only too clear. The Russian's playing was wild, and without change between loud and soft; that of Herr Eck steady, strong but always well-sounding."

We also heard Russian soldiers' songs. "There were six common soldiers, one of whom sang soprano. They shrieked horribly, so that one was tempted to stop his ears. The songs are beaten into them by a sergeant. In some of them they accompanied themselves on a kind of pipe with such a shrill tone that I thought the ladies would faint. The melodies of the songs were not bad, but they were accompanied by all sorts of false harmonies."

Our departure for Riga was delayed until December 2,

as Eck was again unwell. I spent the evenings alternately at the houses of Herr von Berner and Herr von Korf, and played much with Demoiselle Brandt, the young pianist with whom I had assayed the Beethoven sonata. We went through more or less the complete violin and piano repertoire, and I learned to know many masterpieces of Mozart and Beethoven hitherto unknown to me. After dinner we would talk for an hour or so, or I would play chess with Frau von Korf, a game I had loved passionately since childhood.

Herr von Berner, who had taken a great fancy to me, invited me to spend a few months at his country place on my return from St. Petersburg and give some concerts for the Courland aristocracy. I was greatly pleased to learn that I was considered sufficiently advanced to appear publicly as a virtuoso, and accepted with pleasure.

The hour of parting finally arrived, and it was with a heavy heart that I took leave of the families who had taken us in so kindly.

In Riga I found awaiting me a letter from Braunschweig, the contents of which gave me great pleasure. I had asked the Duke's permission to dedicate to him, as my first published work, the new violin concerto, and the letter, from Court Marshal von Muenchhausen, brought me the news of his consent. Impatient to see my work in print, I begged Eck to sponsor its publication with Breitkopf and Haertel, with whom he had connections. The answer came promptly, but was most discouraging. As a consolation to young composers who have difficulty finding publishers for their first compositions, I offer the conditions under which the afore-mentioned house was willing to undertake the publication of my concerto. I had, of course, demanded no payment beyond the receipt of a number of free copies. The firm, however, demanded that I purchase one hundred copies at half the retail price! At first my pride rebelled against such insolent conditions. But finally the desire to have the publication accomplished in time for me to be able to present it to the Duke upon my return to Braunschweig helped me overcome my resistance and accept the condition. The concerto was, indeed, finished in good time, and was already available in Braunschweig upon my return. I couldn't get it however, until I had paid for the purchase of the hundred copies.

In Riga, Eck became entangled in negotiations with the local concert association. The latter, which owned the concert hall, demanded that he play first in one of their concerts, after which they would make the hall and their orchestra available to him. Although this was customary with visiting artists thereabouts, Eck did not wish to comply, and rather preferred not to appear at all. The concert association offered concessions. They would agree if he played with them after his own concert. He agreed on condition that they keep the promise of his subsequent appearance a secret until after he had played, for he had been assured that the local concertgoers, if they knew that they could hear him at one of their own concerts, would be disinclined to patronize a special concert. The secret was not kept, however, and the result was an empty house for his own concert. He was much put out about this and demanded a fee for his appearance at the regular concert of fifty ducats, as compensation for the loss that betrayal of the secret had cost him. The directors, conscious of the justice of his claim, and after long deliberation, offered to settle for thirty. Eck held to his original demand. The directors then threatened to call upon the police to force him to appear, and he was indeed summoned by the local chief of police. The latter, however, became convinced of the justice of his case, and rejected the directors' complaint. Finally, on the day of the concert, after the placards with his name had already been posted, they agreed to pay him the fifty ducats. At this point, however, he declared that, having been summoned by the police, he would not play for double the amount. All threats and imprecations were in vain. The concert was given without him. "I was there," the diary relates, "and enjoyed the ferment among the concertgoers. Everyone spoke of Herr Eck and his refusal to play, but no one had a good word for him. They were all furious about the disappointment. The concert went badly. A flute virtuoso from Stockholm, who played an old-fashioned concerto by Devienne[20] in Herr Eck's place, met with as little approval as a dilletante from St. Petersburg, who played a piano concerto by Mozart in a most studentlike fashion."

Eck had, meanwhile, won the favor of the chief of police by offering to give a benefit for the Nicolai Foundation for the Indigent. The director of the theater placed his auditorium at our disposal, and several local singers volunteered their services. The Musical Association did its best to sabotage the undertaking, but in vain! Eck was greeted with the most enthusiastic applause when he first appeared, and this grew in volume after he had played.

[20] François Devienne (1760–1803), famous French flutist and composer of a method for that instrument. He also played bassoon and oboe.

The receipts were above one hundred ducats after deducting costs. This went to the foundation. But the local gentry who were present got together a purse of one hundred ducats, to which various merchants in town, not wishing to be outdone by the aristocracy, added another fifty the next day.

We left Riga December 17. In Narva the Governor, a great music lover, as soon as he learned of our presence, invited us for the evening. Our protests that we could not appear in our traveling clothes were ignored. The Governor sent his own official carriage for us, and we were brought to him, practically by force. The embarrassment we felt appearing at a brilliant gathering in our rumpled suits was dissolved by the warmth of our reception and the friendly manner of all those present, and we passed a most enjoyable evening. At one o'clock, when the party broke up, we found our own carriage waiting at the door, and continued forthwith upon our journey.

From Narva to St. Petersburg we suffered one mishap after another. "Two stops this side of St. Petersburg we were advised, because of the deep snow, to have runners attached beneath the wheels. But we had proceeded no more than a half hour before the rope, with which the runners were attached, broke, and we could go no farther. The postillion had to fetch some peasants from a nearby village to help him fasten them on again. When the work was done the farmers indicated by signs that we owed them five rubles. Much put out by this outrageous demand, we refused to pay so much. The peasants then surrounded the carriage and made it plain that if we persisted in our refusal they would cut the ropes. As we were in no position to cope with them physically, we had no choice but to pay.

"After a halt of more than an hour we were able to continue, but not for long. We were soon completely stuck in the snow drifts, and required the assistance of a good many more peasants to extricate us. By this time we were convinced that the runners were more of a hindrance than a help, and had them removed. With this accomplished and paid for, we continued on our way. We became stuck seven times more, so that for this single stretch of three miles we required no less than sixteen hours. As we neared St. Petersburg the traveling improved, and we made better time. We finally arrived on Wednesday, the 22nd, at nine o'clock in the evening, having been six days and six nights on the road. We stopped at the Hotel de Londres and promptly engaged a servant, without which it is impossible to exist here. Once you are shown to your room you are left entirely to your own devices."

During the early part of our stay in St. Petersburg, I was much on my own. This would have been the most favorable time for me to become acquainted with the handsome city. But it was simply too cold for sight-seeing. I therefore continued with my studies; indeed, more industriously than ever, as the period of my apprenticeship with Eck was now more than half over. Through a member of the Royal Court Orchestra, we were admitted to the *Buergerklub*, where we met nearly all the artists and intellectuals then living in St. Petersburg. The diary mentions, among others: Clementi,[21] his pupil Field,[22] the

[21] Muzio Clementi (1752–1832), Italian piano virtuoso, one of the most famous musicians of his time. He once competed with Mozart

violinist Hartmann, first violinist of the Court Orchestra, Remi, also of the Court Orchestra, Leveque, son of the concertmaster in Hannover and conductor of Senator Teplow's private orchestra, Baerwald,[23] from Stockholm, the hornist Bornaus, and others.

Clementi, a man in the prime of life, amiable and gay, rather took to me. We spoke in French, which, thanks to much opportunity in St. Petersburg, I now began to speak quite fluently. He often invited me, after meals, to play billiards with him. Evenings I sometimes went with him to his piano store, where Field would be required to play by the hour, in order that prospective customers might hear the instruments to best advantage. The diary speaks glowingly of the superb technique and rather sentimental style of this young artist. I still have a good mental picture of the pale, tall, skinny man, whom I was never to see again. Field had quite grown out of his clothes, and when he sat down at the piano, his long arms stretched out to the keyboard, his sleeves reaching hardly below the elbow, he presented a most awkwardly Anglican appearance. But once his soulful playing began, the listener was all ears.

and confessed to having learned much from the experience. He spent the latter part of his life in London, where he wrote an enormous number of piano compositions, including more than one hundred sonatas and the famous *Gradus ad Parnassum*. Among his pupils were Field, J. B. Cramer, Moscheles, and Kalkbrenner. He became associated with a firm of instrument makers which came to be known as Clementi and Company.

[22] John Field (1782–1837), Irish pianist and composer, pupil of Clementi. After Clementi's departure from St. Petersburg, Field stayed on, prospering both as virtuoso and teacher. His nocturnes strongly influenced Chopin.

[23] Johann Friedrich Baerwald (1787–1861), well-known Swedish violinist, later concertmaster in Stockholm.

Unfortunately the young man spoke only English, and I had to content myself with a handshake as a means of expressing to him how deeply touched I was by his playing.

Many stories were told of the rich Clementi's stinginess, which, when I met him in London in later years, had grown worse rather than better. It was generally understood that he gave Field very little, and that the latter had to pay for his instruction by many privations. I was myself once exposed to a sample of Clementi's thriftiness. Visiting teacher and pupil one day, I found them both at the washbasin, their sleeves rolled up, doing their stockings and other laundry. They refused to be disturbed, and Clementi even advised me to follow their example, as laundering in St. Petersburg at that time was not only expensive but hard on one's clothes.

Of all my new acquaintances, I was fondest of my young friend Remi. A diary entry noting our first meeting, describes him as "a charming and most amiable young Frenchman." Mutual enthusiasm for art, similar studies, and similar tastes drew us closely together. We met every day for lunch at the *Buergerklub*, when my teacher and I were not invited out; and in the evenings, if there were no opera or concert, we would play duets together far into the night. There were a good many such free evenings that winter, for the Emperor, out of consideration for coachmen and servants, had decreed that no public affairs could be held if the temperature fell below seventeen degrees centigrade. This was hard on visitors, and even harder on artists, who had to put up with frequent cancellations and postponements. Eck's public concert, although several times scheduled, could not take place until March 6. In the meantime, however, he played twice at court in the private concerts of the Empress. His second appearance there made such an impression that the Empress had him engaged as soloist of the Court Orchestra with a salary of 3,500 rubles.

The rarer the concert and opera events in the cold months of January and February, the more conscientious was I about attending such as did take place, in order to become acquainted with the native and foreign artists then active. I also saw and heard Tietz, the famous mad violinist. We found a man of forty-odd years, of ruddy complexion and agreeable features. There was nothing about his appearance to suggest mental derangement. Imagine, then, our surprise when he addressed each of us with the question, "My most serene Monarch, what is the state of thy health?" He talked at length without making much sense, complaining bitterly about an evil sorcerer who, envious of his playing, had so hexed the middle finger of his left hand that he could no longer play. He expressed the hope, however, that he would yet succeed in overcoming the spell. As we took our leave, he fell on his knees before Eck, kissed his hand, and said, "My most serene Monarch, I worship the art at thy feet!"

Four months later, at the beginning of May, 1803, all St. Petersburg buzzed with the news that Tietz, whom the Russians, in their blind patriotism, regarded as the greatest violinist of all time, and who, because of his madness, had not played for six months, had suddenly begun to play again. Leveque told me the details. Tietz had been invited to a musicale at Senator Teplow's, but had refused all entreaties to play. Teplow, much put out, dismissed the orchestra and cried, "Then I never wish to hear music again!" This made such an impression on Tietz that he said, "Most serene Monarch, call back thine orchestra, and I shall play a symphony with them." He was as good as his word, and, once under way, played quartets until two o'clock in the morning. The next morning the musical community assembled at his house, and he played again. All this encouraged my own hopes of hearing him, and on May 2 I hurried to his house. Many music lovers were already there, begging him to play, but this time in vain. I heard later that there was someone in the group whom he could not abide.

On May 18 I took my violin and my new duet to Tietz and found him alone. It was not too difficult to persuade him to join me in the duet, although he declined to take the first part. We had hardly finished when some other visitors arrived. Tietz asked me to repeat the duet, and it seemed to please not only him but also the others. At this point, Tietz produced a Haydn quartet, asking me to play first violin. He himself played the cello. It went well, and I was overwhelmed with compliments. Tietz played the second violin part in my duet, which is not easy, without trouble and quite clearly, and managed the melodic passages with taste and feeling. I was less pleased with his scales, which he played in the old-fashioned manner with springing bow.

On May 23 we met Tietz at Senator Teplow's weekly musicale. He played a concerto of his own composition, repeating the first allegro and the rondo, presumably because his performance the first time failed to please him.

The diary says of his playing: "Since, because of his madness, he no longer practices, it is understandable that his technique is insecure. The difficult passages went better the second time. In all three movements he interpolated improvised cadenzas according to the old custom. They were quite attractive, and in the repeated movements wholly different from what had gone before. Tietz is not a great violinist, much less the greatest of all time, as his admirers claim, but he is certainly a musical genius, as is more than clear from his compositions."

During Lent, when no public performances are allowed, the Court Theater gave two big concerts a week in the Steiner Theater, at which all the virtuosos of the Court Orchestra, of which Eck was now a member, appeared. The orchestra, at the first concert, consisted of thirty-six violins and twenty basses and doubled winds. In addition to this, and as reinforcement for the chorus, were forty hornists[24] of the Imperial Band, of whom each individual had to play only one tone. They served as an organ, and gave strength and security to the singing of the chorus, whose parts they doubled. In certain small solo passages the effect was overwhelming. Between the first and second parts of the second concerto, these same hornists

[24] According to Grove, "In 1751 J. A. Maresch, a horn player attached to the court of the Empress Elizabeth of Russia, conceived the idea of forming a band exclusively composed of hunting horns. The instruments varied in length from one foot to seven feet, covered a distance of four octaves, and were thirty-seven in number. Most of the players could only produce the one fundamental tone, but a few of the smaller horns produced two notes. The difficulty of playing with precision by such a band as this must have been enormous; but nevertheless the first concert at Moscow in 1755 was a huge success. Horn bands became the rage with all the great nobles, and they frequently sold the bands—horns and players—to one another."

played an overture of Gluck, with a speed and exactitude that would have been difficult enough for string players and seemed sheerly miraculous as done by hornists, each of them playing only a single tone. It is hardly credible that they could accomplish the most rapid passages with the utmost clarity, and I, for one, would not believe it possible had I not heard it with my own ears. And yet, understandably enough, the adagio of the overture made a greater effect than the allegro for it remains a kind of monstrosity to drill fast passages into these living organ pipes, and one cannot help thinking of the disciplinary methods by which it must have been achieved.

Very popular was a performance of Haydn's *The Seasons*, given for the benefit of the Widow's Fund. Baron Rall, one of the organizers, invited me to participate. I thus played at all the rehearsals and the public performance sharing a desk with Leveque. The orchestra was the largest I had ever heard. It consisted of seventy violins and thirty basses and doubled winds. The effect was magnificent, and the diary speaks of it in glowing terms, as it also speaks of the work itself, which I was then hearing for the first time. I considered, however, *The Creation* to be even greater!

Playing with Leveque had brought us closer together, and I learned from him that he intended to visit his parents in Hannover that summer. We decided, therefore, to go by ship together to Luebeck.

During our now frequent visits with one another, I played my new violin concerto for him and expressed the wish to hear it with orchestra before offering it to a publisher. Leveque immediately volunteered to rehearse

34

it with his own orchestra. He took the score and parts with him, and a few days later invited me to a rehearsal. The diary relates:

"I was terribly excited at the prospect of hearing my composition for the first time with full orchestra. The tuttis were well rehearsed, and I could therefore judge accurately those passages that achieved the intended effect. In most cases I was satisfied, and some passages even surpassed my expectations. . . . I was less pleased with my own playing. Since my attention was directed rather to the accompaniment, I played less well than at home. I therefore asked Leveque if I might not play again in a week or so, when the score and parts would have been copied."

A subsequent entry continues, "Yesterday, I received the copy, which cost me eight silver rubles. In Germany I could have had eight concertos copied for as much."

The work was played through again from the newly copied parts. I was much more at ease than I had been the first time and played far better. The work was also better accompanied and was, accordingly, more effective. Leveque expressed his satisfaction. "I dashed home, packed this concerto up, and carried it off to the post office, only to learn that there was no parcel post to foreign countries in Russia, and that to send my package by letter mail would cost me at least fifty rubles." I withdrew it and subsequently forwarded it by boat.

I mentioned above the Imperial hornists, each of whom has to blow only a single tone. On January 12, at the Emperor's annual New Year's masquerade, to which 12,000 tickets were issued, I found them attached to the dance orchestra, and thus experienced a music of which I had previously had no conception. "The accompaniment of those horns gave the orchestra a fullness and mellowness such as I had never heard before." Certain individual horn solos had an irresistible effect. It was a long time before I could tear myself away.

At a musicale at Baron Rall's I again met the Governor of Narva, who, during our journey through Narva on our way to St. Petersburg, had practically had us brought to him by force. He enquired about my health in the most friendly fashion, and then added, "On your return journey you will find in Narva the Petersburg Gate open and the opposite gate closed, and will be a prisoner at my mercy for eight days."

"At this musicale," reports the diary, "not only Herr Eck but also Field played, and most wonderfully. The guests sat down to dinner at two, and we did not get home until four."

On April 5, my birthday, Eck invited me to lunch at the Hotel de Londres. Previously, the weather being fine, we had taken a walk along the Neva, upon whose granite-walled bank St. Petersburg society was gathered. Everyone was awaiting the breaking of the ice, and many bets were laid as to the day on which this would take place. . . . That evening I had an unexpected and most pleasant surprise. "Remi had again invited me to play duets with him, and I brought along a new one of my own. After we had played it through a second time, he embraced me and said, 'You must exchange violins with me, so that we may both have a tangible remembrance of the other.' I was stunned with joy, for I had long preferred his violin to my own.

But since his was a genuine Guarneri, at least twice as valuable as mine, I had to decline. He refused to be dissuaded, and said, 'I like your violin because I have heard you play it so often. If mine is really better, take it as a birthday present.' I could no longer refuse, and took it home, quite overcome with joy. I should have liked to play it all the night through, and to have indulged myself in its heavenly tone, but as Herr Eck had already gone to bed, I could only let it rest peacefully in its case. But sleep I could not!"

On April 11, Leveque invited me for a walk along the Neva. "We found half of Petersburg there awaiting the breakup of the ice. Finally, a cannon shot from the fortress proclaimed the long awaited moment. This was also the signal for the sailors along the pontoon bridge, connecting Vasilievstrov with this part of the city, to break up the bridge. The ice could now flow out unhindered, and it was not long before boats were moving back and forth. The first of these brought over the Governor of the Fortress, who, accompanied by a numerous retinue and regimental band, proceeded to the Palace, taking to the Emperor a glass of water from the Neva. For this he was rewarded, in accordance with tradition, by a present of 1,000 rubles. Afterwards the royal sailors ferried people back and forth free of charge until the pontoon bridge had been put back in place and normal communications between the two sections of the city restored. . . . After watching all of this for a few hours with much amusement, we returned home."

During the night before Easter, I was awakened by the firing of cannons announcing the opening of the festival. Since it was still very quiet, one could hear each shot repeated in countless echoes. On Easter Day the Russian greets his acquaintances with "Christ is arisen!" whereupon the person greeted kisses the greeter. One had only to go to the window to see embracing and kissing in progress everywhere. They tell the story that Catherine the Great, surrounded by her court, went walking along the Neva one Easter, when a disreputable looking character, probably drunk, accosted her with the greeting "Christ is arisen!" Not wishing to defy the tradition, she had no choice but to kiss him, and did so. But a signal from her sufficed to have the greeter handled less ceremoniously by her guards, and he had ample time afterwards in Siberia to regret his impertinence.

A few weeks later I received from Breitkopf and Haertel a request to describe the state of music in St. Petersburg for their periodical. This appeared in the series of 1803.

The day of our departure drew near. Leveque and I arranged passage with a captain from Luebeck, the trip to cost twenty ducats for the two of us, board included. On June 1 (May 20 by the Julian calendar) I packed my things and set out to say my farewells. The parting from my good friend Remi was particularly difficult, and cost us both many tears. He promised to visit me in Germany. It was difficult, too, to part from my teacher to whom I owed so much, the more so because he had again been suffering from ill health, and I feared that we might never meet again.

This foreboding was well founded. We never saw each other again![25] About his subsequent, often enough highly

[25] Eck died in Strasbourg.

colorful career, I have been able to learn the following, although I cannot vouch for its accuracy, most of it being hearsay.

At the time of my departure from St. Petersburg he was involved in a love affair with the daughter of a member of the Imperial Orchestra, although without the slightest intention of marrying her. Outraged by such irresponsibility, I felt it my duty to warn the girl's parents, and did so. My warning was, however, rather coldly received, and with disbelief. Some months later, after Eck's visits had suddenly ceased, the girl, weeping bitter tears, confessed to her parents that she had been seduced and that the consequences were becoming evident. The mother, a woman of determination, managed to obtain an audience with the Emperor, threw herself at his feet and implored him to see to the restoration of her daughter's honor. The Emperor agreed. With truly Imperial dispatch he gave Eck the choice between marrying his beloved within twenty-four hours or moving on to Siberia. He married her. I can well understand that such a marriage soon became a hell on earth. Eck, whose health was already completely undermined by earlier dissipations, could no longer endure the daily repetitions of marital discord. He lost his mind, and was soon so raving mad that the mother again had to seek assistance from the Emperor. The latter annulled the marriage, awarded the wife a pension, and ordered that the husband be sent, under suitable escort, to his brother in Nancy. The choice of the companion, to whom the wretched Eck and the Emperor's money for the journey was entrusted, turned out to be most unfortunate. No sooner had he reached

Berlin with his demented charge in tow than he announced to the Russian minister there that his funds were exhausted and that he could proceed no further. At the same time he offered the Minister an accounting, according to which the amount approved by the Emperor had, indeed, been expended. Included in the accounting were some extraordinary items, including a dinner for one hundred guests which the mad Eck had given in one of the best hotels in Riga, without the escort's knowledge, and for which the escort had to pay. Whether the Minister was satisfied with this accounting or not remains unknown; the escort, in any case, vanished.

In the meantime the patient, aware that he was no longer being watched, decided to move on. Half clothed, he sneaked out of his room one night, and since it was snowing, managed to get through the city gate unhindered. A few hours from Berlin he was picked up by peasants who, taking him for an escaped criminal, bound him and brought him back to the city. The police quickly recognized the poor, half-frozen fugitive as a lunatic, and delivered him to an asylum. Some members of the Court Orchestra, who had known him and admired him at the peak of his career, did what they could for him. They took up a collection among their colleagues and benevolent music lovers, the proceeds of which were used to send him with a reliable escort to his brother in Nancy. The latter arranged decent accommodation for him in the insane asylum in Strasbourg, where he remained for a number of years. Finally, his former benefactress, the widowed Electress of Bavaria, heard of his plight and sent him to a preacher in or near Offenbach, who specialized in mental disorders. Here he was, if not entirely cured, certainly much improved, at least to the point of being able to play the violin, from which he is said to have drawn touching melodies. Following the death of the Electress, he landed in the insane asylum of Bamberg, where he died in 1809 or 1810.

We set out from St. Petersburg on June 2 (May 21). The diary relates:

"We were stopped by a patrol ship at the mouth of the Neva and required to produce our passports. We received them back without having to pay anything, which, in light of our previous experiences, surprised us greatly. As the wind was against us, the sailors had to row continuously, with the result that our progress was slow and dull, and we were greatly relieved when we finally pulled in at Kronstadt. We stayed at the establishment of a German hotelier of whose trustworthiness we had been assured. In addition to this admirable quality, he possessed less engaging characteristics, among which were coarseness and rudeness, as we learned when, returning from a walk and demanding our supper, we were told, 'This is no time to eat, it's time to sleep.' With which he turned his back upon us and walked away. Completely nonplused, we climbed the stairs and had just about resigned ourselves to the prospect of going to bed hungry, when he suddenly called us down to dinner. Our first impulse was to disdain it, but hunger triumphed over pride. We went downstairs to find a good meal awaiting us. Our host waited upon us himself, and tried in every way to make up for his earlier rudeness."

It was several days before the wind was favorable for

further sailing, but even then we were forced to tack, and by June 14 we were still not far from where we had started. On the second day the sea ran high, and little by little all the passengers, nine men and three women, sucsumbed to seasickness. With me it began with severe headaches. "I felt so miserable that I bitterly regretted ever having gone to sea." On the fourth day I was much better, and soon felt as well as on land, although the sea continued rough. Not all the others were similarly fortunate. The women and some of the men were sick and unsteady for some time. Leveque and I, in the meantime, passed the time pleasantly. We played duets, read, wrote, sketched, walked the deck, and indulged ourselves at the table. Thus one day followed another. Nevertheless, we two prayed for a good wind, "for this eternal tacking, without getting anywhere, is unendurable."

We had a good wind June 15, but on the sixteenth we were becalmed, and on the twentieth there was a storm. This was so severe that the ship creaked in every joint. "Sick as I was, I crawled up on deck to see the awesomely beautiful scene. I was soon soaked to the skin, as the waves were constantly breaking over the bow. What with the cold and the cutting wind, I could not hold out for long. But it was worth all the effort and discomfort to see how the mountainous waves would come rolling on, threatening to engulf us, then suddenly hit us squarely and send us skyward, then roll out from under and drop us into a sickening abyss. Although earlier rough seas had somewhat accustomed me to the spectacle, I still had chills up and down my spine each time this happened, and I would have thought ourselves in grave danger had I not been able to read the contrary in the untroubled countenance of the captain. He gave his orders as phlegmatically as ever. What was frightening, however, was to see the sailors scurry up to the very tips of the masts and slide out on the spars to reef the sails. Only those who have grown up with such dangers can thus cold-bloodedly defy the elements."

June 26 found us off Bornholm, one of the Danish islands. We saw two small towns, many villages, and carefully cultivated farmland. "I rejoiced particularly in the green fields of grain, it having been so long since I had seen anything of the kind." From a neighboring small island "peasants rowed out to our ship bringing fresh meat, milk, and vegetables. The milk was especially welcome, as I could no longer abide the ship's black coffee."

On June 28 we dropped anchor at Travemuende, after a journey of twenty-one days, and on July 5, 1803, I was home in Braunschweig. We arrived at two o'clock in the morning.

"I got out at the St. Peters Gate and hurried to the garden of grandmother's house. Both house and garden entrances were locked, and, as my knocking went unheeded, I climbed over the garden wall, stretched out on the ground in the pavillon at one end of the garden, and went to sleep. There I was discovered next morning by my aunts as they took their morning stroll. They were badly frightened, and rushed back to my grandmother with the news that a stranger was asleep in the garden. Returning with grandmother in tow they ventured closer and quickly enough determined the identity of the mysterious stranger. I was awakened with much embracing

43

and kissing and excited chatter and could not, at first, recall where I was. But then I recognized my beloved relatives and rejoiced to be home again after such a long absence. They had begun to worry about me, having been without news for six weeks."

The first good news I heard was that the famous Rode was in town and would soon play at court. I reported promptly to the Duke, in order to make certain of being able to attend the concert.

At the same time I wrote finis to the much-mentioned diary, expressing the wish that it might "often provide me with pleasant recollections of the wonderful journey."

INTERVAL

SPOHR'S CONCERT AT COURT, at which he was to give evidence of the progress he had made under Eck's tutelage, was a great success, and he was rewarded, not only by the Duke's personal congratulations, but also by promotion to a seat with the first violins, left vacant by a retiring member. This brought with it an increase in salary of two hundred thalers a year, leaving him rather comfortably fixed.

It was not long, however, before he was restless to be off. With the cellist of the orchestra, a Herr Beneke, he departed in the spring of 1804 on a tour whose destination was Paris. It ended abruptly in disaster not far from Braunschweig, however, when Spohr's violin was stolen. There was nothing for it but to return home. A new violin was procured, and on October 19, 1804, he set out on a tour of the German capitals.

II

GERMAN TOUR

(1804–1805)

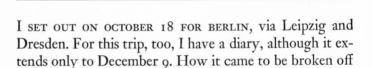

I SET OUT ON OCTOBER 18 FOR BERLIN, via Leipzig and Dresden. For this trip, too, I have a diary, although it extends only to December 9. How it came to be broken off then I shall relate in good time.

My first stop was Halberstadt, where I gave a public concert on October 22 and the next day played for Count Wernigerode. For the public concert the hall was nearly empty, but those present were attentive and appreciative. The program included a symphony by Haydn; my own new Concerto in D minor; the Concerto in D Major by Kreutzer, and the Polonaise from Rode's Quartet in E flat. After the concert, the Count expressed his pleasure and invited me to play for him the next day.

In Magdeburg, too, I was received in the most friendly possible manner. Captain von Cornberg, Major von Witzleben, Regimental Quartermaster Tuerpen, and Counsellor Schaefer, to all of whom I had been commended, did everything possible to assure a good-sized audience and to make my visit agreeable. Even my first concert, on November 3, was well attended. I played my Concerto in D minor, Rode's Concerto in A minor, and his Variations in G.

"Everything went well, and the audience seemed to be carried away by my playing."

"I was invited also to a musicale at the Tuerpens. It was a small but select gathering of the most devoted music lovers of Magdeburg. I played quartets by Haydn, Beethoven, and Mozart, and at the close, the E flat Quartet of Rode. Everything was well accompanied, so that I was able to give all my attention to my playing. The listeners appeared to be delighted. Herr Tuerpen stated that I was able, as no other musician he had ever heard, to play each composition in the style appropriate to it. Finally, our host played a trio by Mozart on an excellent Blum piano. He played well, although with an unfortunate habit of lingering with the melody, by which he did the cause of expression more harm than good."

About my stay in Halle, the next station on my tour, the diary is uninformative. The larger my circle of acquaintances and the more active my social life, the less was I inclined to confide the details to my diary. Or so it seems. Probably I had not the time, for I prepared for every appearance, whether public or private, most conscientiously, and I was also continuously busy with composition. I gave concerts in Halle November 21 and 23, and both were well attended. In addition to my own works, I played Rode's Concerto in A minor and the

G Major Variations. According to the diary, "my playing was enthusiastically received."

Among those who were helpful in arranging my concerts was the famous contrapuntist Tuerk.[1] He conducted
the Academy Concerts, one of which took place during
my stay. This was a concert production of Mozart's "La
Clemenza di Tito." The audience had been assembled for
half an hour. The orchestra was tuned up, and awaited
the signal to begin. But one of the singers was missing,
a vocal teacher who was to take the part of Tito. When
he finally arrived, the students in the audience broke into
general hissing and booing. The singer, into whose hands
the conductor had already pressed the music, stepped forward and, with a contemptuous expression, said, "If you
don't like me, you can get along without me." With that
he threw the music at the conductor's feet and stomped
off. Some effort was made to catch him and bring him
back, but all in vain!

I now assumed that the concert would be postponed,
or at least that the numbers involving Tito would be cut.
Not at all! The conscientious conductor deprived his
listeners of not one measure. On his little harpsichord he
played the entire part of Tito, recitatives, arias, and ensembles, from the first note to the last. I was nonplused,
hardly knowing whether to be angry or to be amused.
One thing, however, that evening made clear to me: One
can be a learned contrapuntist and still be without a shred
of taste.

[1] Daniel Gottlob Tuerk (1756–1813), composer and author of important theoretical works. Carl Loewe, the great German ballad composer, was his pupil.

GERMANY (1815–1914)

I arrived in Leipzig November 29. The diary offers two brief reports of this visit and then expires into silence forever. The first discusses a production of Paer's[2] opera *Die Wegelagerer*. The second describes a visit to a *Gewandhaus* Concert.

"The concerts," the diary recounts, "are arranged by a society of merchants. They are, however, by no means amateur concerts. The orchestra is composed exclusively of musicians, and is both large and good. The vocal soloist

[2] Ferdinando Paer (1771–1839), prolific Italian opera composer, none of whose operas have survived. *Die Wegelagerer (I Fuorusciti)* was produced in Vienna in 1804.

is always a visiting artist, since the local theater director will not permit any of his singers to appear at these concerts. This year's soloist is a Signorina Alberghi from Dresden, daughter of a Dresden choir singer.[3] She is still very young, but has already a good method and a clear, resonant voice. She sang two arias with great success. I also heard the concertmaster of the society, Herr Campagnoli,[4] play a concerto by Kreutzer, and quite well. His technic is old-fashioned, to be sure, but he plays clearly and securely. The hall in which these concerts are given is very beautiful, and most favorable to the musical effect."[5]

In the arrangement of my own concert, I had many difficulties to overcome. With all the busy activity of this trading center, people were not as helpful to me as I was by now accustomed to, and I had much to do before all the obstacles had been removed. I was also rather piqued to find that the rich businessmen, to whom I had been commended, appeared to know nothing of my accomplishments. My reception was friendly enough, but rather cool. I was most anxious therefore to be invited to a musicale, where I might have occasion to draw attention to myself. This wish was fulfilled. I was invited to a large evening musicale with a request to play something.

I chose for this occasion one of the loveliest of the six new quartets of Beethoven, in the performance of which I had often delighted my audiences in Braunschweig. In

[3] Ignazio Alberghi, tenor at the Dresden Opera and composer of church music.

[4] Batholomeo Campagnoli (1751 – 1827), concertmaster of the *Gewandhaus* Orchestra at Leipzig.

[5] The concert hall described by Spohr endured only until 1885. Thereafter the concerts were removed from the *Gewandhaus* (Cloth Hall) to a new building.

the very first measures I noticed that the accompanying players were unfamiliar with this music and, therefore, unable to play it with the proper spirit. This was bad enough, but I was considerably more disturbed when I noticed that the audience was paying little attention. Conversation began which soon became so loud that it drowned out the music. I sprang from my chair, even before the end of the first movement, and hurried to my case to pack my violin. This caused a great sensation among the gathering, and our host approached me questioningly. I went straight to him and said in a voice loud enough to be heard by all, "I am accustomed to being heard attentively. Since this has not been the case here, I can only assume that I would please the assemblage by departing." The host was at a loss for an answer and withdrew in embarrassment. When, however, after making my apologies to the musicians, I started to leave, the host returned and said in a perfectly friendly way, "If you could see fit to play something else, something more appropriate to the taste and capacity of this gathering, you would find a most attentive and grateful audience." Since it had already dawned upon me that in choosing music ill-fitted for such a gathering, I, too, was to blame, I was only too happy to comply. I took the violin from its case and played Rode's Quartet in E flat, which the musicians knew, and which they accompanied well. There was now absolute quiet, and I could sense the interest in my playing increasing with each movement. At the end of the quartet there were so many flattering compliments that I was prompted to trot out my war horse, Rode's G Major Variations. With this I so delighted the audience that I was the subject of the most flattering attention for the remainder of the evening.

This incident was much talked of for several days and probably accounted for the fact that many music lovers, thus made aware of my presence, turned out for the rehearsal of my concert. On this occasion, by my performance of my Concerto in D minor, I made such an impression that, even before the concert, I had established a considerable reputation. Thus, the concert proper attracted a much larger audience than I should otherwise have dared to hope. It was the elite of the Leipzig musical public, and a most receptive audience. I so succeeded in arousing their enthusiasm that a second concert was demanded. This took place eight days later, and drew one of the largest audiences ever to attend a concert by a visiting artist in Leipzig. In the meantime I was invited to a number of quartet evenings, where, having first rehearsed them with my accompanists, I played my favorites, the first six quartets of Beethoven. I was the first violinist to play them in Leipzig, and succeeded, through my manner of playing them, to win them full recognition. At these quartet evenings I met the editor of the *Musikalische Zeitung*, Court Councillor Rochlitz,[6] and maintained the friendliest relationship with him until his death. Rochlitz reviewed my concerts in his paper. As this review established my reputation in Germany and had considerable influence upon my career, I may be pardoned for reproducing it here:

[6] Johann Friedrich Rochlitz (1769–1842), one of the first of the great German music critics and founder of the *Allgemeine Musikalische Zeitung*, published in Leipzig.

"Herr Spohr gave a concert in Leipzig on December 10, 1804, and a second, in response to many requests, on December 17. In both concerts he afforded us a stimulating pleasure such as we have not enjoyed from any other violinist within our memory, with the possible exception of Rode. Herr Spohr ranks without doubt among the finest of living violinists. One would be astonished at his achievements, particularly at so tender an age, could such sheer pleasure permit of cold astonishment. He offered a large concerto of his own composition (D minor), which he had to repeat, and a second, also of his own composition (E minor). His concertos are among the most beautiful in existence. With respect to the Concerto in D minor particularly, we know of no other violin concerto to compare with it, either for invention, substance, and charm, or for exactness and thoroughness. His individuality inclines him toward grandeur and a sentiment lightly touched with melancholy. This applies also to his playing. Herr Spohr can manage anything, but it is these characteristics that are most compelling. What we think of as correctness in playing in its widest significance is with Herr Spohr, as a solid foundation, only a point of departure. Perfect purity, security, precision, the most brilliant finish, every type of bowing, all varieties of violin tone, the most natural ease in the execution of all such things, even in the most difficult passages—these render him one of the most skillful of virtuosos. But the soul that he breathes into his playing, the flight of fantasy, the fire, the tenderness, the intimacy of expression, the good taste, the insight into the spirit of the most varied compositions, and his ability to present them each in its own style and spirit—all this makes him a true artist. This last quality we have never had occasion to admire in any other violinist in the same degree. This applies especially to Herr Spohr's quartet playing. It is no wonder, then, that he is everywhere admired and leaves nothing to be desired except that he remain and provide ever new opportunities for the enjoyment of his playing."

This made me very happy! But it was not alone the recognition I had achieved as an artist that occupied my thoughts. There was another and tenderer sentiment. I loved and was loved.

The day after I first saw and heard Rosa Alberghi at a *Gewandhaus* concert, I paid her a visit in order to invite her to participate in my own concert. Mother and daughter received me in a most friendly manner. The former, although she had lived in Germany a good many years, had not learned a single word of our language. Since she only shook her head at my attempts to communicate in French, I had to address my request to her daughter, who had grown up in Dresden and spoke German fluently. She accepted readily, and chatted on with childlike lack of self-consciousness as if we were old acquaintances. As I took my leave, Rosa urged me to come soon again. I had already looked too deeply into her fiery black eyes to delay acting on the invitation, and was soon spending most of my free time with her. I accompanied her vocal exercises at the piano, as best I could, helped her prepare the pieces sent to her by the concert management, and adorned her arias with new ornaments, in which she always found a truly childlike pleasure. Thus our relationship, almost without our being conscious of it, became

54

steadily more intimate. Rosa sang again in my second concert, and since her contract in Leipzig was coming to an end, and she was about to return to Dresden, she offered to appear again in my concert there.

Armed with excellent introductions, I moved on to Dresden. A letter from Rosa introduced me to her father, who welcomed me most warmly. He and several members of the Dresden Court Orchestra helped me with the arrangements for my concert and thus eased this ever disagreeable duty.

Rosa returned to Dresden a few days before the concert, and participated in it, along with her father. The success, both of my compositions and my playing was as great as it had been in Leipzig. As in Leipzig, I was widely urged to give a second concert. While this was being arranged, I was advised to present myself at court since, in view of the excitement my playing had aroused, there could be no doubt of a favorable reception. When I learned, however, that the court concerts took place during dinner, and that no exceptions were made even for visiting artists, my youthful artist's pride rebelled at the thought of playing to the sound of clattering dishes, and I forthwith renounced the honor of being heard.

My second concert was extraordinarily well attended, and the applause almost more enthusiastic than at the first.

It was time to think of my departure for Berlin, but the thought of separation from my beloved Rosa was so painful that I could not bring myself to it. At this point her father surprised me with a proposal that deferred the dreaded separation. He said that he had long wished that Rosa might appear in Berlin, and that if I were agreeable to the idea of having her appear in my concert, he would send her along in the company of her mother, he himself being unable to obtain leave.

I agreed readily enough, and commenced making the travel arrangements. As the trip by post was considered too trying for the ladies, we joined in the rental of a private carriage. I thus sat opposite my sweetheart and had no complaints about the length of the journey. Arrived in Berlin, we found rooms in a house discovered for us by my old teacher Kunisch, now a member of the Berlin Court Orchestra, to whom I had previously written. The latter, not a little proud of being able to introduce the young artist as a former pupil, arranged introductions to Berlin's most distinguished artists, and was most helpful in preparations for the concert. There were so many concertizing artists in Berlin at the time, however, that this event had to be considerably postponed.

In the meantime I delivered my letters of introduction and was invited, accordingly, to a number of musicales. I played first at the home of Prince Radziwill,[7] who was an excellent violinist and a talented composer. There I found Bernhard Romberg,[8] Moeser,[9] Seidler, . . . and other distinguished artists. Romberg, then in the prime of his virtuosity, played one of his quartets with cello obbligato. I had never heard him before, and was delighted with his playing. Urged to play myself, I could think of nothing worthier of such artists and connoisseurs than my

[7] Prince Anton Heinrich Radziwill (1775–1833).

[8] Bernhard Romberg (1767–1841), a cousin of Andreas Romberg and himself a cello virtuoso and composer.

[9] Karl Moeser (1774–1851), Berlin violinist and conductor. He conducted the Berlin premiere of Beethoven's Ninth Symphony.

beloved Beethoven quartets. Again it was brought home to me, as earlier in Leipzig, that this was a mistake; for the Berlin musicians were as little acquainted with these quartets as the musicians of Leipzig, and knew neither how to play them nor how to appreciate them. When I had finished, they praised my playing, but spoke disparagingly of what I had played. Romberg even went so far as to say, "But my dear Spohr, how can you play such baroque stuff?"

I began to have doubts of my own taste, hearing one of the most distinguished artists of the time speak thus of my favorite quartets. Later on, when asked to play again, I chose, as at Leipzig, the E flat Quartet of Rode, and enjoyed a similar success.

The second musicale, to which my traveling companion was also invited, was given by Prince Louis Ferdinand of Prussia.[10] We went to his palace together and were most cordially received by our host himself. We found an elegant group of bemedaled gentlemen and well-groomed ladies, as well as the best artists of Berlin. And there I met a former acquaintance from Hamburg, the pianist and composer Dussek, who was now the Prince's teacher in residence. The musical program began with a piano quartet, which he played with true artistic perfection. I followed. Enlightened by my recent experience, I chose only pieces with which I could shine as a violinist, namely a quartet and the G Major Variations of Rode. My playing was much applauded, and Dussek, especially, seemed to

[10] Prince Louis Ferdinand of Prussia (1772–1806), a nephew of Frederick the Great and a pupil of Dussek. He was killed in battle at Saalfeld, October 10, 1806.

be impressed. Rosa, too, accompanied by Dussek in an aria, found general approval.

When the musical program had come to an end, the Prince offered one of the ladies his arm and led the assemblage into the dining room, where a magnificent meal awaited us. One took one's place beside one's lady without regard for protocol. I sat next to Rosa. The conversation, although free and unembarrassed, was, at first, respectable enough. But when the champagne began to flow, it began to include utterances unfit for the chaste ears of an innocent maiden. As soon as I noticed that the elegant ladies present were not, as I had at first assumed, from the court, but more probably from the ballet, I made plans to sneak away with my young companion. Somehow we managed to escape unnoticed to my carriage, and I returned with Rosa to her anxiously waiting mother. Next day I was told that the Prince's musical parties commonly ended with such orgies.

I remember still a third musical party—at the banker Beer's[11]—when I heard the now famous Meyerbeer, then a thirteen-year-old youngster, play under his parent's roof. The gifted boy, even then, excited such admiration by his virtuosity on the piano that his relatives and co-religionists regarded him only with pride. The story was told that one of them returned from a lecture on astronomy and cried: "Just think of it, they have ranked our Beer among the stars! The professor showed us a group of stars named 'The small Beer,' in his honor."[12]

[11] Meyerbeer's real name was Jakob Liebmann Beer. His father, Herz Beer, was a wealthy Berlin banker. He received a legacy from a relative named Meyer and attached the latter's name to his own, thus becoming Meyerbeer.

I had the good idea of inviting the young virtuoso to play a solo at my concert, and the invitation was accepted by the family. Since this was the boy's first appearance, it drew a crowd of his coreligionists and it was largely due to this circumstance that mine was one of the best attended concerts of that overcrowded season. After many obstacles had been cleared away, it finally took place in the foyer of the theater. My playing, as also the singing of my traveling companion, was received, as in Leipzig and Dresden, with much applause. Less favorable was the review of the *Musikalische Zeitung,* recently founded by *Kapellmeister* Reichardt.[13] The latter, in his singularly biting manner, took exception particularly to my indifference to strict tempo. Although piqued by such criticism, to which I was not accustomed, I had to admit that, influenced by my deep feeling, I dragged in the cantilenas and rushed in the big passages and other passionate episodes. I undertook, therefore, insofar as it was possible without sacrificing expression, to cleanse my playing of such deviations, and with continued attention to the problem, I succeeded.

After several futile attempts to arrange a second concert in Berlin, I had to give up the project. I therefore divided the not inconsiderable proceeds of the first concert with my traveling companion and began to think about returning to Braunschweig, as my leave was coming to an end. Rosa's mother was also anxious to return to Dresden, as her efforts to obtain an engagement for her

[12] A play on words, the German "beer," as in Meyerbeer, being pronounced similarly to "Baer" (bear).

[13] Johann Friedrich Reichardt (1752–1814), composer and critic, publisher of the *Berlinische Musikalische Zeitung.*

daughter with the Italian Opera in Berlin had not been successful. Rosa had become ever more devoted to me and made no effort to conceal her affection for me. I, on the other hand, as I had come to know her better, was convinced that she was unsuited to be my companion for life, and had carefully avoided any declaration. She was, to be sure, a lovely, unspoiled child, and richly endowed by nature. Her education, however, aside from the social amenities, had been much neglected. I was particularly annoyed by her bigoted piety, which had, on several occasions, prompted attempts on her part to convert the Lutheran heretic to Catholicism. I bore up under the parting with commendable composure. Rosa, however, dissolved in tears, and, during our final embrace, pressed into my hand a piece of cardboard with the initial "R" sewn into it from her own beautiful black hair.

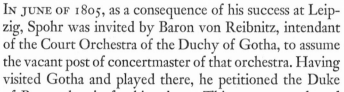

INTERVAL

In June of 1805, as a consequence of his success at Leipzig, Spohr was invited by Baron von Reibnitz, intendant of the Court Orchestra of the Duchy of Gotha, to assume the vacant post of concertmaster of that orchestra. Having visited Gotha and played there, he petitioned the Duke of Braunschweig for his release. This was granted, and he accepted the new position at a salary of about 500 thalers a year, plus allowances. He entered upon his new duties in October, 1805.

These duties consisted of the arrangement of a court concert every week, winter and summer. The local circumstances permitted ample time for rehearsal, and things went well. The orchestra was composed partly of court musicians, partly of court oboists, the latter having the additional duty of playing at table and at court dances. There were also two court singers. One of the latter, a Madame Scheidler, had a daughter, Dorette, a harpist, whom Spohr married on February 2, 1806. Throughout their life together she accompanied him on all his tours and appeared as assisting artist in most of his concerts. To provide material for her participation, he wrote a number of pieces for violin and harp.

The first group of these, including a Concertante for Harp, Violin, and Orchestra and a Fantasy and Variations for harp alone, were composed in preparation for a tour of German cities which began in the summer of 1807, shortly after the birth of their first child, a daughter whom they named Emalie. For this tour, Spohr had a carriage specially constructed to accommodate the harp and the violin, as well as the two passengers.

III

SECOND GERMAN TOUR

(1807–1808)

THE JOURNEY BEGAN INAUSPICIOUSLY, when, on the very first day, our carriage turned over on the stretch between Erfurt and Weimar. Fortunately, neither we nor our instruments were damaged, and we suffered no more than the fright. On no other of our many journeys did we have any further accident of this kind.

In Weimar, where we arrived with letters of introduction from the Duchess of Gotha, we played at court with great success, and were generously rewarded by Grand Duchess Maria. Among the audience were the two great poets, Goethe and Wieland. The latter appeared to be utterly carried away by our playing, and expressed himself in the friendliest manner. Goethe, too, dignified and cold, honored us with words of praise.

As I see from a report in the *Musikalische Zeitung,* we gave a concert in Leipzig on October 27. The verdict on my compositions, namely, the overture to *Pruefung*,[1] the Violin Concerto in E flat, the first Concertante for Harp and Violin, the Potpourri in B flat and the Harp Fantasy was very favorable. As to my playing it stated:

"We have spoken before of the playing of Spohr and his bride, and shall add here only that he has entirely freed himself of certain liberties (in rhythm, etc.) for which he has been criticized in the past, and now ranks without doubt among the best of all living violinists, both in *allegro* and *adagio*, (in our opinion particularly in the latter); Madame Spohr, thanks to her technical accomplishment and the charm and graciousness of her playing, is certain to have a distinguished success."

I remember little of Dresden. We gave a concert there and played at court, although certainly not for the table, to which neither of us would have consented. Of Prague, on the other hand, I remember a good deal. My reputation had not extended that far, and I had, at first, to contend with many difficulties. These were resolved when we played at a soiree of the Princess von Hohenzollern and she undertook to be our patroness. We were immediately fashionable, and society flocked to our two public concerts. We had every reason to be satisfied with our stay, as is attested further by the following extract from a report in the *Musikzeitung:*

"The third (among the visiting artists) was the well and favorably known concertmaster of the ducal orchestra at Gotha, Herr Spohr, who was heard on the violin, as was his wife on the harp. Not soon will another

[1] *Die Pruefung*, Spohr's first opera, completed in 1806, but except for a concert performance in Gotha, never given.

artist have occasion to be so completely satisfied with his reception, and every music lover will testify that the distinction was well-earned."

In the further course of his review, however, this critic found much to criticize in my playing, a verdict in which he seems to have been alone. Of the concert of the Pixis brothers, which followed mine, he said of the violinist, "He had to take a place far below Spohr," adding, "since everyone had been so delighted by Spohr's playing just a few days before, and Pixis' playing was judged accordingly, the verdict was not entirely just."

From Prague we continued on to Regensburg and Munich. I no longer remember whether we played at Regensburg or not. If so, I have been able to find no report of it. And even our appearance in Munich is recorded only briefly in a review of the season in the *Musikalische Zeitung*. "Herr Spohr of Gotha gave a concert here and was well received." I, however, remember the visit vividly. Before giving our public concert, we played at court. As we came forward to play our Concertante for Harp and Violin, we found no chair for Dorette. King Max,[2] who was sitting with the Queen in the first row, noticed this, and before a servant could bring one, he promptly offered his own gilded and crowned armchair. In his amiable manner he insisted upon her using it, and would not be dissuaded until I pointed out that the arms would be a hindrance to her playing. When we had finished our program he himself presented us to the Queen and her en-

[2] Probably Maximilian I Joseph (1756–1825), elector of Bavaria, who gained territory by the Treaty of Pressburg and, by its terms, assumed the title of king in 1806.

tourage, all of whom conversed with us most pleasantly. Next day we received the royal emoluments, a ring of brilliants for me, a diadem for Dorette, both very valuable.

From Munich we journeyed to Stuttgart, armed with letters of introduction to the court. I presented these to the court marshal and next day we received assurances that we would be heard. I had learned, however, in the meantime, that the court played cards during the playing and that little attention was paid to the music. Still shuddering from my experience with such degradation of art at Braunschweig, I took the liberty of declaring to the court marshal that my wife and I would play only if the King would desist from card playing during our offerings. Horrified at such audacity, the court marshal took a step backward and exclaimed, "What! You presume to give orders to my most serene master? I would never dare to convey such a message!"

"Then," I replied, "I must forego the honor of being heard at court," and took my leave.

How the court marshal ever brought himself to deliver my message, and how his majesty took it, I never learned. But the result was a message from the court marshal which ran as follows:

"His Majesty graciously deigns to comply, but only on condition that the pieces be played one after the other so that His Majesty need not be inconvenienced more than once."

And so it was. After the court had seated itself at the card tables, the concert began with an overture, followed by an aria. While these were being performed, the servants moved about noisily, serving refreshments, while the card players called out their "I bid," "I pass!" so loudly that nothing much could be heard of the music. Then the court marshal came over to me and told me to be ready to play. He then announced to the King that the visitors were ready to present themselves. The King arose, as did all the rest. The servants set up two rows of chairs, and on these the court took their places. Our playing was listened to attentively and in silence. There was not even any applause, for no one dared to anticipate the King, and the latter contented himself with a gracious nod at the conclusion of each piece. When we had finished, our audience hustled back to the card tables, and things continued noisily as before. As soon as the King had finished his game, he pushed his chair back and the concert was broken off in the middle of an aria by Madame Graff, the poor lady having to stop with the last note of her cadenza still in her throat. The musicians, accustomed to such vandalism, quietly put their instruments away in their cases, but I remained outraged at such a performance.

Wuerttemberg suffered in those days under a despotism, the like of which has hardly been known elsewhere in Germany. Anyone, for instance, who arrived at the palace in Stuttgart had to make the journey from the outer gate to the palace portal with bared head, despite rain or snow, because His Majesty's apartments were on that side. Every civilian, moreover, was required by royal order to take his hat off to the sentry, although the latter was not required to acknowledge the courtesy, At the theater, applause was forbidden unless the King himself applauded. The royal family however, because of the winter cold, kept their hands in muffs, and brought them out only when they felt the urge to take a pinch of snuff. At such moments, they also applauded, regardless of what was going on in the theater. The chamberlain, who stood behind the King's[3] seat, would then join in, thus giving the cue to the loyal subjects that they should also applaud. It was almost always the most interesting scenes and the finest pieces of music that were thus disturbed.

As the people of Stuttgart had long grown accustomed to complying with the royal whims, there was no little astonishment when word got around of the conditions I had exacted and gotten for my appearance at court. This drew attention to me, with the result that my public concert was extraordinarily well-attended. The Court Orchestra supported me most obligingly, and its conductor, Danzi, assisted me in every possible way with the arrangements. Danzi was, indeed, a remarkably decent fellow, and I felt especially drawn to him because of our mutual admiration of Mozart. Mozart and his works were the inexhaustible subject of our conversations, and I still possess a precious souvenir of that time, a four-hand arrangement of Mozart's Symphony in G minor, transcribed by Danzi himself and in his own hand.

It was in Stuttgart that I first made the acquaintance of the subsequently so famous Carl Maria von Weber,[4] and established a friendship which endured until his death. He was then secretary to a Prince of Wuerttemberg and only avocationally concerned with music. This did not prevent him from composing at a great rate, and I still

[3] King Friedrich I (1754–1816). He had been Duke of Wuerttemberg since 1797 and king since 1806, thanks to Napoleon. He died in 1816.
[4] Weber was secretary to Duke Louis, brother of King Friedrich.

remember hearing, as an example of his work, some numbers from the opera *Der Beherrscher der Geister*. These struck me as so insignificant and so dilettantish that I certainly did not dream that Weber would one day produce an important opera. However, I was measuring all dramatic music in those days against Mozart.

I remember nothing in particular about the concerts we gave in Heidelberg and Frankfurt am Main prior to our return home. A clipping from a Heidelberg newspaper speaks of my playing in "the style of Rode." This surprised me at the time, for I thought that I had left Rode far behind me. Because there was only a small accompanying orchestra, I had played a Rode concerto, and this may have had something to do with it. About the concert in Frankfurt on March 28, the *Frankfurter Zeitung* reported that we had been "very enthusiastically received."

Approaching Gotha we were ceremoniously met a few hours from town by a group of my students and escorted home. Dorette's relatives were gathered to greet us, and we found our daughter in the best of health, thanks to her grandmother's loving care. As our journey had earned us, not only applause, but also what was for us a considerable sum of money, we could feel well-satisfied with our fortune.

INTERVAL

A SECOND DAUGHTER, IDA, WAS BORN TO THE SPOHRS on November 7, 1808. Shortly after her confinement, Dorette suffered an attack of pneumonia which nearly cost her her life. Her recovery was slow, and upon the physician's advice, Spohr rented a villa with a garden, where his wife would be assured of fresh air and restful surroundings. By mid-summer of 1809 she was so far recovered that a new tour was contemplated. Spohr composed a new large Sonata for Harp and Violin (Opus 115) in preparation for it. Dorette worked it up, and by October they were ready to be off.

IV

THIRD GERMAN TOUR

(1809–10)

THUS RE-EQUIPPED FOR THE NEW TOUR, we began to consider an itinerary. From a traveler recently returned from Russia, I learned that our fame had penetrated there and that our visit had already been anticipated in St. Petersburg the previous winter. As I could, moreover, count upon influential recommendations from the court at Weimar to the court of the Czar, Russia seemed to be a promising destination. Dorette, however, was reluctant to journey so far from home and to be separated from the children for such a long time. I argued that, if we were ever to get to Russia, now was the time, while the children were still small enough to be cared for by their grandmother, and too young to miss us. She tearfully agreed. Since I realized in advance that the Duchess would also be reluctant to grant me leave for such a long time, I kept quiet about our Russian destination. I asked and received a three-month leave to go to Breslau. From there I intended to press for an extension.

We set off in October, 1809, played in Weimar, and received there from the Grand Duchess our letters of introduction to her brother, Czar Alexander, and other notables. Then we played a concert in Leipzig, about which the *Musikalische Zeitung* wrote: "Herr Spohr and his wife gave us the pleasure of an entire evening of his violin playing and his newest compositions, as well as the pleasure of hearing his wife at the harp. We have previously had occasion to speak in detail of this fine artist and his gifted wife. We may content ourselves here with the observation that both have made remarkable progress since we last heard them, both technically and in the art of putting their virtuosity to artistic use. And if the compositions of this master have previously excited admiration here and elsewhere, of these most recent examples we can only say that they will be even more admired."

I have searched in vain for reports of our concerts in Dresden and Bautzen, and know no more than that they took place on November 1 and 7, and this only from the financial records of our journey. About our concerts in Breslau, November 18 and December 2 and 9, I have a review of the *Musikalische Zeitung*, which speaks favorably of our playing but finds some fault with the compositions. It says: "The verdict of our music lovers on Herr Spohr as a composer is in accordance with verdicts previously passed on him. He is certainly a fine composer. Characteristic of his new compositions, however, insofar as we know them, and even to the point of one-sidedness, is their melancholy mood. Even the Potpourri that he played at the end had more than a trace of it." This observation about the melancholy character of my compositions, the first of its kind that I can remember, has been echoed many times since, and remains a mystery to me. The great majority of my compositions seem to me fully as cheerful as those of any other composer. Particularly those which I played in Breslau, with the exception of two movements, are of such a cheerful character that I am at a loss to explain the observations quoted above.

We found in Breslau an old friend from Gotha, the former intendant of the Court Orchestra, Baron von Reibnitz, who had retired to his estate in Silesia. He had come to town for the winter and knew everyone who had anything to do with music in Breslau. He introduced me into the local musical community, and was most helpful to me in the arrangements for my concerts. Breslau, traditionally one of the most musical of German cities, had so many concerts at that time that one took place almost every weekday. Since the theater also played every day, it was not easy to find suitable dates, and still harder to get together a good orchestra. I surmounted these difficulties with the assistance of Herr Schnabel,[1] musical director of the Cathedral, who not only assembled the orchestra for each of my three concerts, but also conducted it. This experienced conductor approached my compositions with an affection which he soon extended to the composer, and which the latter most cordially reciprocated. We became fast friends, and remained so until his early death.

[1] Joseph Ignaz Schnabel (1767-1831).

Shortly after my arrival in Breslau, and just as I was about to request the extension of our leave in order to continue on to Russia, I received, through Baron Reibnitz, a communication from Count Salisch, the court marshal in Gotha, to the following effect: From Weimar, the Duchess had learned to her sorrow of my intention to continue on to Russia, thus extending my leave to after the first of the year. As she was most unhappy to have me and my wife absent from the Court Concerts for such a long time, she proposed, by way of compensation, if I would forego Russia and return to Gotha, to engage my wife as soloist for the Court Concerts and as music teacher for the Princess.[2] When my wife learned of the contents of the letter I could see how the hope of being reunited with her children brought tears of joy to her eyes. This touched me so deeply that I promptly decided to forego the Russian tour. Instead, I began negotiations with Count Salisch, now also the intendant of the Gotha Orchestra, and when these resulted in the engagement of my wife at an appropriate salary, effective January 1, 1810, I promised on my own part to return to Gotha with all possible speed. We hastened our departure from Breslau, and traveled via Liegnitz to Glogau, where, on December 13 and and 18, we gave very well-attended concerts, arranged in advance by local music lovers. From there we continued on to Berlin.

The city was full of visitors, all awaiting in a great state of excitement the return of the court, which had been in

[2] The Princess was the Duchess' stepdaughter. She later married the Duke of Coburg and became the mother of Prince Albert of England.

residence in Koenigsberg since the fateful battle of Jena. It was a good time for concerts. Even our first concert, which took place before the arrival of the court, was well-attended. The correspondent of the *Musikalische Zeitung* reported: "Herr Spohr played his Concerto in G minor, with the Spanish Rondo, a Potpourri, and, with the assistance of his accomplished wife, a Sonata for Harp and Violin, also of his own composition. The *Musikalische Zeitung* has frequently had occasion to praise this talented virtuoso and, more recently, his compositions, too. Here, also, we had both virtuoso and composer. We particularly admired the double-stops, the leaps, and the trills, which Herr Spohr executes with the utmost security, and with his expressive playing, particularly in the adagio, he won his listeners' hearts as well as their admiration. We hope to hear this distinguished couple again next week."

The festive return of the court took place January 10. It was, indeed, a moving spectacle, the King, his Queen beside him,[3] moving slowly in his open coach through the crowded streets, acknowledging the acclamations of a thousand voices, with flags and banners waving from every window. The Queen was deeply touched, the tears streaming down her cheeks from her beautiful eyes. That evening the city was brilliantly illuminated. We gave our second concert the following day. Early in the morning we were overwhelmed with inquiries as to whether the court would attend. At first we ourselves did not know. But about noon, when the Queen sent for tickets, the

[3] King Frederick Wilhelm III and Queen Luise.

news spread through the city like wildfire, and people came in such droves that the hall could hardly accommodate them.

I had originally intended to go from Berlin directly to Gotha, in order to keep my promise. A music lover from Hamburg, however, told me that this would be a favorable time to play there, so I asked Gotha for a few weeks' extension, which was granted.

At that time Hamburg was occupied by the French, who were carrying out a blockade against England. The local merchants, still very rich, had little to do, and, therefore, leisure for music. Our reputation had preceded us, and even our first concert, given in the Apollo Hall on February 8, drew a large audience at a high price of admission. As our playing at this concert created a sensation, we did even better at the second, on February 21. Between two Hamburg concerts, we gave one on the fourteenth in Luebeck. We gave a final concert at a suitable fee at the Museum in Altona.

Thoroughly satisfied with our profits, we were set to depart, when the secretary of the French governor appeared and invited us, in behalf of the governor, to play still a third concert, as he and his staff had not yet heard us. I was afraid that a third concert might not draw well, and was prompted to decline when the secretary interjected that the governor and his staff would take two hundred tickets. All my reservations were therewith dissolved, and we gave a third concert on March 3.

In Hamburg I made the personal acquaintance of Andreas Romberg[4] and the musical director, Schwenke.[5]

Both these famous artists received me cordially, and were most helpful in arranging my concerts. Romberg saw to the assembling of a good orchestra, and conducted it himself, while Schwenke, the dreaded critic, saw to the placement of announcements in the newspapers. Since his judgments carried the utmost authority, the favorable terms in which he introduced us to the public and, later, discussed our performances, contributed not a little to our great success. Both artists led pleasant family lives, and took pleasure in having us to tea. On such occasions the talk was only of music, much of it both instructive and amusing. There was a lot of quartet playing in Hamburg at that time, and Romberg had his quartet, whose special ornament was the cellist, Prell,[6] beautifully trained. It was a pleasure to join them. Romberg played only his own quartets, and while no great virtuoso on his instrument, played them easily and with taste. However, he never really warmed to his work, as evidenced by the fact that he could smoke his pipe while playing. I played his favorites among the Mozart and Beethoven quartets and, here too, attracted much favorable attention by my ability to adjust my style to that of the composer. Schwenke was most complimentary on this point. At his request, I was required to play two of my own quartets. I did so re-

[4] Andreas Romberg (1767–1821), well-known violinist and composer. He succeeded Spohr in Gotha in 1815.

[5] Christian Friedrich Gottlieb Schwenke (1767–1822), organist, pianist, and composer, a pupil of C. P. E. Bach. He has gone down in history as one who dared to rescore *The Messiah* and Bach's Mass in B minor.

[6] Johann Nikolaus Prell (1773–1849), cellist and chamber musician in Hamburg.

luctantly, as they no longer met the standards that I now set for this form. I said as much, but they found favor nevertheless, even with the critical Schwenke. Only Romberg dissented. He said to me with engaging forthrightness: "Your quartets don't amount to anything; they are not on a level with your orchestra pieces." Although I agreed, still, it annoyed me to hear this judgment from another. So it was that when, some years later, in Vienna, I wrote some quartets which seemed to me worthier than my other works, I dedicated them to Romberg in order to show him that I could now write quartets that "amounted to something."

Returning in good spirits to the comparative quiet of Gotha, I was distressed only by the thought that the Duchess might be displeased by our long absence, and this anxiety was hardly relieved when the Duchess declined to receive our courtesy call. We saw her first at the Court Concert. As I well knew that the best way to get back into her good graces was to appear promptly at one of these concerts, my wife and I played one of my sonatas, which I followed with the Duchess' favorite Variations in C Major by Rode. This had the desired effect, and after the concert the Duchess came to us, greeted us most cordially, and would not even hear our apologies to the end. Thus reassured, we could enjoy to the full the pleasure of being reunited with our children.

INTERVAL

In the spring of 1810, Spohr accepted the directorship of a music festival in Frankenhausen, the participants to be drawn from singers and instrumentalists from the principal communities of Thuringia. This festival, which may well have been the founding father of the innumerable festivals that have taken place in Europe since then, was built around a performance of *The Creation* and a symphony concert. The program of the symphony concert is worth noting as an example of what was offered in those days: a New Grand Overture for Full Orchestra, by Spohr; a Grand Italian Scena, by Righini[1]; a New Concerto for Clarinet, especially composed for this occasion by Spohr; an organ improvization as introduction to the final chorus in C Major from Haydn's *The Seasons;*

[1] Vincenzo Righini (1756–1812), Italian opera composer and director, who spent the greater part of his distinguished career in the German courts. He was a pupil of Padre Martini.

79

a double Concerto for Two Violins, by Sophr; a Grand
Rondo from a Concerto in D Major, by Romberg, and,
finally, the Symphony in C Major, by Beethoven. A newspaper account of the concert refers to "Herr Spohr's conducting with the role of paper,[2] accomplished silently and
without grimaces." For a second festival the following
year, Spohr not only directed again but also contributed
his First Symphony, especially commissioned for the
occasion.

Following the first festival, Spohr completed an opera,
Der Zweikampf der Geliebten, which had been commissioned in Hamburg during his recent visit to that city. He
completed it in the winter of 1810–11, and it was put on,
after many vicissitudes, in Hamburg on November 15.
It was a success, but Spohr was not pleased with it. Much
more gratifying was his first oratorio, *The Last Judgment*,[3] done on commission for a festival in honor of Napoleon's birthday, in Erfurt on August 15, 1812.

The tour to Vienna, which began in the autumn of
1812, had entirely unexpected consequences, among them
a change of residence and place of employment from
Gotha to Vienna. Since, however, the new residence and
the new employment turned out to be less permanent than
was at first anticipated and since this period was most
fruitful in terms of experience, the Vienna episode is
treated here as one of the journeys.

[2] Spohr was one of the pioneers of modern conducting. The use of
the roll of paper was a transitional device between the earlier use of
the concertmaster's bow and the later use of the baton.

[3] *The Last Judgment (Das Juengste Gericht)*, not to be confused
with his later and better-known oratorio, *Die Letzten Dinge*, also
known in English as *The Last Judgment*.

V

JOURNEY TO VIENNA

(1812–15)

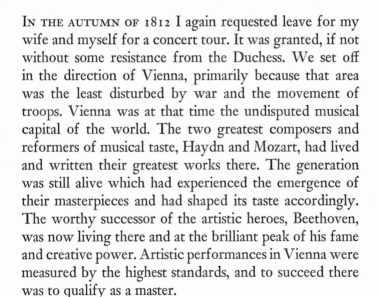

IN THE AUTUMN OF 1812 I again requested leave for my wife and myself for a concert tour. It was granted, if not without some resistance from the Duchess. We set off in the direction of Vienna, primarily because that area was the least disturbed by war and the movement of troops. Vienna was at that time the undisputed musical capital of the world. The two greatest composers and reformers of musical taste, Haydn and Mozart, had lived and written their greatest works there. The generation was still alive which had experienced the emergence of their masterpieces and had shaped its taste accordingly. The worthy successor of the artistic heroes, Beethoven, was now living there and at the brilliant peak of his fame and creative power. Artistic performances in Vienna were measured by the highest standards, and to succeed there was to qualify as a master.

I felt my heart beating faster as we crossed the bridge over the Danube and I thought about my approaching debut. My anxiety was intensified by the thought that I would have to compete with the greatest violinist in the world, for I had learned in Prague that Rode had just returned from Russia and was expected momentarily in Vienna. I still remembered vividly the overpowering impression that Rode's playing had made upon me ten years before in Braunschweig, and how I had struggled for years to adopt his method and interpretive style. I was therefore most anxious to hear him again and measure my own progress accordingly. My first question as I climbed down from the carriage was whether Rode had arrived. I was told that he had not, but that he had been expected for some time.

It behooved me to appear before his arrival, and I hastened with the preparations for my concert. I was successful in making the arrangements, but in the meantime, I learned that Rode had arrived and was going to attend the concert. To my surprise I found this reassuring rather than distressing, and played my very best. The *Musikalische Zeitung* wrote: "On December 17 we had the pleasure of admiring Herr Louis Spohr and his wife in a concert. This reviewer is happy to endorse the verdicts previously rendered about this couple in the *Musikalische Zeitung* and can only add that their masterly playing charmed everyone. Herr Spohr played a Violin Concerto with a Spanish rondo, and at the end of the concert a Potpourri, both of his own composition. With his wife, he played a Sonata for Pedal Harp and Violin, of which he was also the composer. Both were works of some significance, a far cry from the watery, hastily put together things offered by so many executive artists, with neither talent nor calling for composition."

On the advice of well-wishing friends, I decided against giving my oratorio at my own expense, as I had originally intended, the cost of a large orchestra and chorus being so much greater than the usual cost of a concert that I could not have hoped to earn anything. I still considered this work one of the finest of its form, however, and was most anxious to give it a hearing. I proposed, therefore, to the Society of Widows and Orphans to produce it for them as a benefit, my only condition being a large orchestra, chorus, and solo group, selected from the best musicians in Vienna. The Society agreed, getting together an ensemble of three hundred of the city's best artists. The work was carefully prepared in two general rehearsals and went better than any previous performance.

I was delighted anew with my creation, an enthusiasm shared by many of the participating musicians, particularly the conductor of the *Theater an der Wien*, Herr Clement.[1] The latter had so identified himself with the work that, on the day following the performance, he played several larger numbers for me on the piano note for note, with all progressions and orchestral figures, and this without ever having seen the score. Clement had a musical memory equalled, possibly, by no other artist. They told me in Vienna that after hearing Haydn's *Crea-*

[1] Franz Clement (1780-1842), famous Viennese violinist and conductor, for whom Beethoven wrote his violin concerto.

tion several times he had it so perfectly from memory that, with the help of the text, he made a complete piano score. When he brought it to old Haydn, the latter's first impulse was to assume that someone had stolen his score or had secretly copied it. After examining it carefully he found it so accurate that he accepted it for publication.

Before my oratorio could be performed I had a bout with the censors. They would not tolerate the use of the names Jesus and Mary either in the cast of characters or over the parts they were to sing. Not until the names had been expurgated would they permit the printing of the text. After offering considerable resistance I finally agreed, since the content made it easy enough to determine who was concerned.

Although the oratorio pleased the musicians and increased my stature as a composer in their eyes, its success with the public was by no means comparable to the success I enjoyed as a violinist and composer for the violin. There was no want of applause, but the enthusiasm was not sufficiently general to draw a full house to the second performance, three days later. This second performance was the last ever given. In later years I became so aware of its weaknesses and deficiencies that I could not bring myself to perform it again.

Two weeks after my first appearance came Rode's concert. Thanks to his European reputation he could engage Vienna's largest concert hall, the *Redoutensaal*, and fill it. I awaited Rode's playing with feverish excitement, but even in his first solo it appeared to me that it had fallen off. I now found his playing cold and mannered, and missed the former daring in the mastery of difficulties. I was particularly disappointed in his playing of the cantabile passages. The public seemed to share my disappointment; at least Rode was unable to stimulate much excitement.

Eight days after his concert I gave my second in the small *Redoutensaal*. The *Musikalische Zeitung* reported: "Spohr fully established himself as a great master of the violin. In the tender and agreeable, he is unquestionably the nightingale of all the living violinists of our acquaintance. It would hardly be possible to play an adagio at once so tenderly and so distinctly, and all with the utmost refinement. In fast tempi he masters difficult passages, including the most extended reaches, with incredible ease, thanks partly, no doubt, to the size of his hand. He was again enthusiastically and unanimously applauded, and was repeatedly recalled, an honor which we can remember being accorded previously only to Herr Polledro."[2]

Thus I had every reason to be content with my reception in Vienna. I was also fully recognized and appreciated in private gatherings, where, as a rule, I met and competed not only with Rode and other visitors, but also with the best of the local violinists, Herr Mayseder.[3] At first there was always a dispute as to who should begin, as each wished to be last, in order to overshadow him who had gone before. I, however, always preferring a fine quartet to playing solos, never refused to begin, and was

[2] Giovanni Battista Polledro (1781–1835), one of the great Italian violinists. He was also a composer and conductor.

[3] Joseph Mayseder (1789–1863), Viennese violin virtuoso, chamber musician, and composer of chamber music.

always able, due to my individual approach to the classic quartets, to attract the attention and approval of the audience. When the others had paraded their war horses, and if I noticed that the listeners preferred this kind of thing to classical music, I would bring out one of my difficult and brilliant potpourris, and was usually able to outdo the bravura performances of my competitors.

With these frequent opportunities to hear Rode, I became ever more convinced that he was not the perfect violinist he once had been. Through the constant repetition of ever the same pieces, his playing had become mannered to the point where it bordered on caricature. I had the rudeness to suggest as much to him once by asking if he could remember how he had played his own pieces ten years ago, and then added insult to injury by getting out his Variations in G Major and proposing that I play them for him in exactly the way I had heard him play them when I had first heard him. When I had finished there was an ovation, and even Rode, if only for form's sake, had to contribute his "Bravo." I noticed, however, that my indelicacy had hurt him, and quite understandably. I was thoroughly ashamed of myself, and mention the incident only as an indication of how sure I was of myself as a violinist in those days.

Utterly satisfied with Vienna, I had begun to think of our further journey when Count Palffy,[4] the owner of the *Theater an der Wien*, quite unexpectedly offered me

[4] Count Ferdinand von Erdoed Pallfy (1774–1840), member of an aristocratic Hungarian family. The *Theater an der Wien* still stands. It housed the Vienna *Staatsoper* from 1945 until the opening of the new *Staatsoper* in 1955.

a three-year engagement as conductor and concertmaster.
I was reluctant to give up my own and my wife's lifetime
engagement at Gotha, and at first declined. But Herr
Treitschke,[5] who handled the negotiations, then offered
me three times our combined salaries at Gotha. He told
me, moreover, that Count Palffy had succeeded in engaging the best living singers and that he now wished to
entrust to me the building of an orchestra from the finest
musicians in Vienna, in short that the *Theater an der Wien*
would shortly be the best in Germany. He also told me
that I would have an opportunity to develop and distinguish myself as composer for the theater. I could not
resist so much temptation, and asked for a little time to
discuss it with my wife.

With this salary, which was considerably more than
that earned by either Salieri[6] or Weigl,[7] the court conductors, I could hope to save at least a third and possibly
even half. With the reputation I enjoyed now in Vienna,
I could, moreover, count on adding a good deal to my
income by concerts, composition, and teaching. Even if
the engagement should end after the three years, I would

[5] Georg Friedrich Treitschke (1776–1842), poet, actor, and theater
director in Vienna. He did the textual revision of *Fidelio* for the revival
of 1814.

[6] Antonio Salieri (1750–1825), one of the most celebrated Italian
composers of his time. The greater part of his career was centered in
Vienna where he was for twenty-four years director of the Court
Opera. Haydn, Gluck, Beethoven, and Schubert all thought highly of
him, the latter two sufficiently so to solicit his instruction. Mozart was
his rival at the opera, and Salieri was at one time suspected of having
poisoned him, a rumor long since discounted.

[7] Joseph Weigl (1766–1846), Viennese opera composer and conductor and for many years Salieri's assistant at the Court Opera.

be secured for the immediate future, and could realize my childhood dream of a trip to Italy with my wife and children.

More persuasive than anything else was my desire to write for the theater. And so, with Dorette's consent, given with much concern at the prospect of separation from mother and family, I signed the contract. I undertook to act as concertmaster at all important operas, to play the violin solos for operas and ballets, and to conduct from the score when the other conductor was unable to do so. I was released from smaller operas, ballets, and incidental music for the spoken drama. I conferred now with Count Palffy and my new colleague, the conductor von Seyfried,[8] about the reorganization of the orchestra. The Count was by no means niggardly about salaries, and it was not difficult in a short time to get the most gifted musicians and to assemble an orchestra that was not only the best in Vienna but also one of the best in all Germany.

In signing my contract I had exacted a four-week leave in the spring to straighten out my affairs in Gotha and to pick up our children. Before that, however, I had to find a place to live in order that we might set up housekeeping upon our return. In this connection there occurred something that was to influence not only the question of a place to live but also my artistic career in Vienna. Word had hardly gotten around Vienna that I was to settle there when, one morning, a distinguished visitor

[8] Ignaz Xaver Seyfried (1776–1841), Vienna opera composer, conductor, and critic, pupil of Haydn and close friend of Mozart and Beethoven.

presented himself: a Herr von Tost,[9] manufacturer and passionate music lover, excusing the importunity of his visit by explaining that he had a proposition. After he had taken a seat and I had seated myself expectantly opposite him, he began a hymn of praise about my talent as a composer, and expressed the wish that, for a suitable emolument, everything that I should write in Vienna be reckoned as his property for a period of three years. I was to give him the original manuscripts and make no copies. At the end of three years the manuscripts would be returned to me, and I would be free to publish them or dispose of them in any other way that I saw fit. After considering this curious proposal for a minute, I asked if this meant that the works were to remain unperformed during the period of his ownership. Tost replied, "Oh, no! They may be performed as often as possible, but the score must be borrowed from me for each occasion and performed only in my presence." Nor did he wish to prescribe the form of the composition, although he would prefer works suitable for performance in private circles, such as quartets and quintets for stringed instruments, and sextets, octets, and nonets for strings and winds. I was to think it over and myself determine the fee for each form of composition. With this he presented his card and took his leave.

My wife and I attempted in vain to fathom the motive of this proposal, and I finally decided to question him

[9] Johann Tost, a rich textile manufacturer from Moravia and one of the founders of the Vienna *Gesellschaft der Musikfreunde*. Haydn dedicated some quartets to him under a similar arrangement.

directly. First, however, I made some inquiries about him, determining that he was a rich man, the owner of a cloth factory in Znaim, and a great lover of music who never missed a public concert. This was reassuring, and I decided to accept this proposal. As fee for the three-year suspension of my rights, I set thirty ducats for a quartet, thirty-five, for a quintet, and so on for the other forms. When I asked him just what he proposed to do with my works for three years, he was reluctant to answer, observing that this should be a matter of indifference to me as long as he was pledged not to publish them. However, when he noticed that I was not satisfied with this, he added: "I have two objectives. First, I want to be invited to the musicales where your pieces will be played, and therefore I must have them in my possession. Secondly, I hope that on my business trips the possession of such treasures will bring me the acquaintanceship of music lovers who, in turn, may be useful to me in my business."

While all of this did not make much sense to me, I had to admit that it indicated a high estimate of the value of my compositions. I found this most pleasantly flattering, and I had no further reservations. Tost accepted the fees that I had set, and further agreed to pay upon delivery. The appropriate documents were drawn up and signed accordingly. I had brought with me to Vienna the manuscript of a solo-quartet for violin, which I had finished on the journey, and had begun a second. I decided to finish the latter and present the two of them to Tost before my departure for Gotha.

In the meantime I had managed to find a suitable apartment, right near the *Theater an der Wien,* on the first floor of a carpenter's house. As the apartment was rather shabby, I had had it cleaned and painted and was now about to furnish it. As this would involve a considerable outlay, I delivered my two quartets to Tost and asked for the fee of sixty ducats, explaining that I needed the money for the furnishing of my apartment. "I will provide everything," he exclaimed, "and more cheaply than you could get it for yourself, for I have business connections with all the people with whom you would have to deal, and can get better prices than you. At the same time it will give me an opportunity to collect some old debts. Name a day when I may pick you both up, and we will make a shopping expedition together."

And so it was. First we drove to the apartment, where Tost expertly drew up a list of what would be needed. Then we went from one shop and warehouse to another. My wife and I had our troubles preventing him from buying mahogany furniture, upholstered in silk, for the dressing room, not to mention silk drapes. He assembled a collection of kitchen utensils and table service that would have been more fitting for a capitalist than for an unpretentious artist. Dorette protested without avail that we would not be entertaining and had no need of such finery. He was not to be deterred, and when I protested that all this would be beyond our means he replied, "Don't worry; it won't cost you much, and I shall not require cash. You can pay it all off with your manuscripts." There was nothing more to do about it, and thus we found ourselves in possession of an elegant and tasteful establishment, which no other artist family in the city could match.

I now arranged my departure. My wife was invited to stay with a lady of our acquaintance, the sister of a lawyer named Zizius, a great music lover at whose house we had often played. Thus I had no anxiety about leaving her behind.

I had learned that a Leipzig salesman, returning home in his own carriage, was looking for a traveling companion. I hastened to offer myself as such, and we soon came to terms. His name escapes me, but I remember him as a cultivated, sympathetic companion. We traveled without stopover to Prague, but remained there for a day to recover from the journey. Leaving Prague, we were forced to deviate from the main Dresden road because the combatant powers were facing each other there, and the bridge over the Elbe was unpassable, the French having blown up one of its arches. We had to find our way over the Erzgebirge. There were detachments of troops here, too, but we were neither halted nor turned back. Thus we arrived without further incident at Chemnitz. Here I was to have an adventure that was to cause me to faint, for the first and last time in my life.

We arrived in Chemnitz about noon, at a time when a numerous crowd was gathered at the hotel for lunch. We joined the crowd, and I found a place at the table between my traveling companion and the proprietress of the hotel. While the latter was serving the soup, I followed the example of the rest of the company and started to cut a piece of the big chunk of black bread placed before each of us. I plunged the knife into the bread, but made no progress, since, as it later developed, it came against a small bit of stone that had been baked into the bread. At first, however, I thought that the knife was dull, and pressed down upon it with redoubled strength, whereupon it sprang back and cut off a piece of the index finger of my left hand. There was a stream of blood. The sight of the blood, or rather the thought that this might be the end of my violin playing and that I would no longer be able to support myself and my family, was such a shock that I fell unconscious from my chair. When I came to, some ten minutes later, I found myself surrounded by the whole company, all excited and much concerned about me. My first glance was for my finger, now bound up in a single piece of court plaster, provided by the helpful proprietress. It was set deeply into the cut, and I was relieved to learn that the whole fingertip had not been cut away, as I had feared during the initial shock. But a good half of it was gone, along with a substantial bit of nail. As I felt hardly any pain, I left the bandage as it was. I looked up a doctor in Leipzig, and he, too, left the bandage untouched, advising only the careful avoidance of any hard knocks.

Thus, relatively reassured, I returned to my family and friends in Gotha. I found the Court highly displeased about our move to Vienna. The Duchess was so angry that I had some difficulty in calming her, the more so because I could not make a farewell appearance at Court, which she had fervently desired. I hastened to remove myself from this unpleasant situation as quickly as possible. I had, some weeks before, commissioned my old friend, Baerwolf, to sell such furniture and equipment as I would be unable to take to Vienna, and in this he had been successful. What remained, mostly beds, mirrors, music, clothes, underwear, etc., I had allowed to be packed and shipped ahead by freight to Regensburg. Eight days later, accompanied by my brother, Ferdinand, my two children, and a servant girl, an orphan whom my mother-in-law had taken in and raised, I departed for Vienna.

The parting from my relatives and my beloved Gotha was a sad one. But, with the assistance of good traveling weather, our spirits were soon restored, and I found particular pleasure in the naïve comments of my children about all that was new to them. We arrived, tired but happy, in Regensburg. We stayed there a few days while I made arrangements for our further journey down the Danube to Vienna. For a moderate price I engaged a private boat and had our freight brought on board. The beds were unpacked and set up for sleeping under the wooden pilot house. The trunks served as seats. Since the trip was to be without stopover, we loaded provisions for four or five days. The ship's company consisted, not counting ourselves, of the boatman, his wife, who took care of the cooking, the ship's boy, and three young workmen who received travel and board in return for serving as oarsmen.

It was in May, with the moon full, and the deep blue sky extended infinitely over the magical countryside. Spring had just clothed everything in the loveliest green, and the fruit trees were in full bloom. The verdant banks of the splendid river were inhabited by countless nightin-

Louis Spohr, self-portrait.

Spohr's birthplace, Braunschweig, Spohrplatz 7, as it looked at the time of his birth and as it still looks today. It was one of the few buildings in Braunschweig to survive World War II unscathed.

Stadtarchiv, Braunschweig

gales, who, particularly during the moonlit nights, sang continuously. It was an utterly charming journey. Time and again since then I have tried to make the trip under similarly favorable circumstances, but in vain.

When we arrived at the famous rapids and whirlpool,[10] which could not be navigated without some danger in those days, our heretofore jovial boatman became quite serious and admonished the oarsmen to follow his instructions to the letter. At the moment when the roaring stream struck the boat, he turned pale, and his wife fell to her her knees, bawling rather than speaking a prayer to the Virgin Mary. Even to me the moment seemed to be fraught with peril. I even advised my brother who, like myself, was a good swimmer, to stand by to rescue the children in case of a mishap. However, we came through the steep rapids right side up and avoided the whirlpool, which is, in fact, really dangerous only for very small boats. On the big rock which stood at the end of the rapids and caused the whirlpool there lived at that time an old hermit, who survived from the donations of travelers. He rowed out to us in his little boat, much to the delight of the children, who had never seen a hermit before, and received his customary reward.

We reached Vienna toward evening of the fourth day, and found Dorette, in the company of her hostess, awaiting us at the landing. That was a happy reunion! Our

[10] The Danube rapids—between Linz and Vienna below the city of Grein. The rocky island, which caused the dangerous whirlpool, was called Hausstein. It has since been removed.

baggage was brought to our new apartment that same evening, and next day we moved in.

By the time of our arrival in Vienna my finger was' nearly healed. To my astonishment, and even more to the astonishment of the doctor to whom I told the story, new flesh had formed under the court plaster, in which the finger was still bound, and now entirely filled the area of the fingertip that had been cut away. The missing piece of nail had also been renewed, although not without an unevenness that has remained until this day. With the help of a leather covering, I could now use the finger again and play in the orchestra, although I could not immediately resume my duties as soloist.

I led a busy and happy life. Early morning found me either at the piano or at the writing desk; and, indeed, every other time of day not taken up with orchestral duties or teaching was devoted to composition. My head was so full of music that even on the way to my pupils or during my walks, I was mentally composing. I soon developed the capacity of working out long periods and even whole compositions in my head, which I could write down afterwards without further reflection. As soon as this was done, the music vanished from my memory, leaving room for new combinations. Dorette often complained about this during our walks, and was happy when the chatter of the children distracted me from my continuous concentration. Once this had happened, I could devote myself just as wholeheartedly to external impressions, and Dorette always managed tactfully to prevent my falling back into my musical reveries.

During that first summer in Vienna we became well acquainted with the city's lovely surroundings, as we spent every free evening out of doors. We would take our simple supper with us in a basket and seek out some advantageous point from which to watch the sunset. On Sundays we would take a little wagon and make longer expeditions to the Leopoldsberg, Laxenburg, and Baden, etc. The children's favorite trips were to the menagerie at Schoenbrunn, or to the Prater, to the so-called "little village" where the carousel, the dog and doll theater, and other novelties never ceased to delight them. My wife and I, both still half-children, participated wholeheartedly in their pleasure. It was a lovely, gay, carefree time.

My first undertaking after returning from Gotha was the composition of *Faust*. From the catalogue of my compositions I see that I finished this opera in less than four months, from the end of May to the middle of September. I still remember with what enthusiasm and endurance I worked. As soon as I had a few numbers finished I would rush off to Meyerbeer, who was living in Vienna at that time and who was a marvelous score reader. He would play the orchestral score and I would sing the vocal parts. What my voice could not manage, I whistled, which I did well. Meyerbeer took great interest in the work, an interest which appears to have persisted, since during his regime at the Berlin opera he prepared a new production of it.

Pixis, the younger, who was then living in Vienna with his parents, as well as Hummel and Seyfried, showed a great partiality for this work, and I had high hopes for a brilliant success when I offered it to the *Theater an der Wien*. Count Pallfy, with whom I was still on good terms, accepted it without hesitation, and promised to get it into production as soon as possible. In writing *Faust* I had kept the singers of our ensemble in mind. As it turned out, I still did not understand how to keep within bounds of normal vocal range, and had written all kinds of things that did not suit the singers. Count Pallfy used this afterwards, when we had reached the parting of the ways, as an excuse for having broken his promise of a production. Indeed, it was never given in Vienna during the period of my residence. It was given some years later with great success, and a new production was mounted recently even more successfully. Having always been interested in my works only while at work on them, I took this setback casually and went to work on new compositions. Not until many years later did I bother even with a publication of the piano score, which had been affectionately prepared by Pixis.

After finishing *Faust* I bethought myself of my obligations to Tost, and asked him what he would like. He thought for a moment and decided for a nonette, made up of four strings plus flute, oboe, clarinet, horn and bassoon, to be written in such a way that each instrument would appear in its true character. I was much attracted by the difficulty of the assignment and went right to work. This was the origin of the famous Nonet, published by Steiner in Vienna as Opus 31, which remains to this day the only work of its kind. I finished it in short order and delivered it to Tost. He had it copied out and then invited the best artists in Vienna to his house to try it out under my direction. It was played at one of the first musicales of the new season and aroused such enthusiasm that it was repeated frequently in the course of that same season. Tost appeared each time with the score and parts under his arm, set them out on the music stands himself and gathered them up again after the performance. He was as pleased by the applause as if he himself had been the composer. The two quartets which I had given him in manuscript were also played frequently, and thus his wish to be invited to many musicales was amply fulfilled. Indeed, people became so accustomed to seeing him with his scores under his arm whenever I played that they began to invite him even when I was playing pieces of mine that did not belong to him.

Before the end of the year 1813, I wrote a Rondo for Harp and Violin for my wife and myself and a string quartet for Tost. This was the Quartet in G Major, Opus 33.[11] This quartet involved me in a literary feud, the first and last that I ever fought in behalf of one of my compositions. The quartet was very well received by the artists and connoisseurs of Vienna, and I regarded it as the best thing of its kind that I had written. Thus, I was especially annoyed when the critic of a Vienna art periodical of the time could find nothing good to say about it. I felt particularly insulted by what he said about the theoretical working out of the first movement, which was my special pride, and which had excited the admiration of the connoisseurs. To this day I can remember more or

11 Spohr's memory failed him. It is a string quintet.

less exactly the words he used: "This eternal mastication of the theme in all voices and in all positions reminds one of a master giving an order to a servant which the latter is too stupid to grasp and which the master therefore repeats countless times and with every variety of vocabulary, idiom, and inflection in order to make it absolutely clear. The composer seems to regard his listeners as just this type of stupid servant."

I soon learned that the anonymous critic was von Mosel,[12] composer of a lyric tragedy, *Salem*, of which I had once said loudly, "In all my life I have never heard anything so unutterably boring!" This judgment had, unfortunately, been brought to the ears of the composer, and had annoyed him considerably. Tost, who was prouder of my compositions, particularly of those in his possession, than the composer himself, insisted that I render a rebuttal. What I said in my defense, and particularly in defense of my thematic elaboration, I no longer remember, although it certainly was not lacking in appropriate references to *Salem*. This was oil in the fire, and led to a feud that would have gone on and on had not the censor cut it off by forbidding the editor of the periodical to print anything further on the subject. As such quarrels were most distasteful to me, I was only too happy to return to my harmless composition.

Shortly after my arrival in Vienna I had looked up Beethoven. He was not at home, and I left my card. I

[12] Ignaz Franz von Mosel (1772–1844), Viennese composer and critic and, like Spohr, a pioneer in conducting with the baton. He conducted the first of the festivals of the *Gesellschaft der Musikfreunde* and was one of the three chief mourners at Beethoven's funeral.

hoped to encounter him at one of the musicales, to which
I was frequently invited, but soon learned that Beethoven,
now that his deafness had reached the stage where he could
no longer hear music distinctly and coherently, withheld
his presence from all musicales and had become generally
shy and withdrawn. I tried again to pay a call, but in vain.
Finally, I met him unexpectedly in the restaurant where
my wife and I lunched every day. I had already appeared
in a concert, my oratorio had been twice performed, and
the Vienna press had been favorable in its commentary.
It was not, therefore, as an unknown that I introduced
myself, and Beethoven greeted me with unusual cordial-
ity. We seated ourselves at a table, and Beethoven became very talkative. This occasioned much surprise in
the room, as he usually sat, staring straight ahead, dour and
silent. It was uphill work trying to get anything across
to him, as one had to shout loud enough to be heard two
rooms away. Thereafter, Beethoven used to come frequently to this restaurant, and he also visited me in my
apartment. Thus we became good acquaintances. He was
a bit rough, not to say uncouth, but an honest eye peered
out from beneath his bushy brows.

After my return from Gotha I used to meet him now
and again at the *Theater an der Wien*, where Count
Pallfy had provided him with a free seat right behind the
orchestra. He would accompany me home after the performance and spend the rest of the evening with me. On
such occasions he was always most engaging with Dorette
and the children. Of music he rarely spoke. When he did,
his judgments were very severe, and pronounced with a

finality that seemed to exclude any thought of contradiction. In the work of others he showed not the slightest interest, and I had not, therefore, the courage to show him mine. His favorite subject at that time was what he conceived to be the iniquities of the theater administrations of Prince Lobkowitz and Count Pallfy. About the latter he thundered his imprecations while still in his theater, and in such a manner as to be heard, not only by the departing audience, but also by the Count himself in his office. This caused me some embarrassment, and I was always at some pains to change the subject.

Beethoven's coarse, even repulsive behavior of those days stemmed partly from his deafness, which he had not yet learned to bear with resignation, and partly from his ruinous financial circumstances. He was a bad manager, and had the additional misfortune to be robbed right and left by those around him. He often lacked the barest essentials. In the early days of our acquaintanceship I asked him once, after he had been absent from the restaurant for several days, "Have you been ill?" He replied, "It was a shoe, and as I have but one pair I had a few days house arrest." He was rescued from this appalling situation some time later by the efforts of his friends. It happened in the following manner:

Fidelio, which had had only a slight success when produced under unfavorable circumstances during the French occupation of Vienna in 1805, was now remounted by the *régisseurs* of the *Kaerntnerthor Theater* and produced for their benefit. Beethoven was persuaded to write a new overture (the overture in E), a song for the prison warden, and the great aria for Fidelio (with horn obbligato), as well as to undertake a few alterations.[13] In this new form the opera had a resounding success and experienced a long run to full houses. At the first performance the composer was recalled again and again and was once more the object of general attention. His friends took advantage of this favorable moment to organize a concert for him in the large *Redoutensaal*, at which his newest compositions were to be played. Everyone who could play, blow, or sing was invited to participate, and none of the more important artists of Vienna were missing. I and my orchestra were, of course, among them, and I had my first experience of Beethoven's conducting. Although I had heard a good deal about it, the actuality still came as a shock. Beethoven had adopted the habit of communicating his expressive desires to the orchestra by all sorts of odd movements of the body. For a *sforzando* he would throw apart his arms, hitherto held crossed on his heart. For a *piano* he would bend down, the more *piano*, the lower. Then at a crescendo he would rise up gradually, and at the onset of the *forte*, literally spring into the air. He often shouted, too, in order to contribute to the *forte*, although probably unconsciously.

Seyfried, to whom I expressed my astonishment at this extraordinary way of conducting, told me of a tragicomic incident which had occurred at Beethoven's last concert in the *Theater an der Wien*.[14] Beethoven was

[13] The song of the Prison Warden and Fidelio's aria date from the original version.

[14] The Beethoven Concert took place December 8, 1813. The occa-

playing a new piano concerto and at the first *tutti* forgot that he was soloist, jumped up, and began to conduct in his own inimitable manner. At the first *sforzando* he flung his arms so wide apart that he knocked both candlesticks from the music rack on the piano. The audience broke out laughing, and Beethoven was so incensed by the disturbance that he had the orchestra begin again from the beginning. Seyfried, anxious lest the same thing happen again, summoned two choirboys and had them hold the candlesticks in their hands next to Beethoven. One of them came close to the piano and peered unsuspectingly into the piano score. As the fateful *sforzando* arrived, Beethoven fetched him such a blow on the mouth with his outwardly swiping right hand that the poor boy dropped the candlestick to the floor. The other boy, more cautious, had been following Beethoven's movements most closely, and managed to duck in time. The initial laughter now became sheer hilarity. Beethoven fell into such a rage that he broke half a dozen strings on the first chord of his solo. The efforts of the true music lovers to restore order and attention were of no avail, and the first allegro went pretty much unheard. Since this incident, Beethoven had been reluctant to give concerts.

This concert arranged by his friends, however, was a most brilliant success. Beethoven's new compositions were extraordinarily well liked, particularly the Symphony in A Major (No. 7), whose wonderful second movement had to be repeated. It made a deep and enduring impres-

---

sion referred to by Seyfried is presumably one that took place December 22, 1808, when the Concerto in G Major had its first performance.

sion upon me. The performance was absolutely masterly, despite Beethoven's uncertain and often ridiculous conducting.

It was quite plain that the poor, deaf master could no longer hear the softer passages of his music. This became particularly apparent during a rehearsal in a certain passage in the second part of the first movement, where there are two successive closes, the second of them *pianissimo*. Beethoven apparently overlooked this, as he began to beat the time before the orchestra had even attacked this second close. Thus, all unknowingly, he was ten or twelve measures ahead of the orchestra when the latter began, and *piano* at that. In order to indicate the *piano*, Beethoven had practically crawled under the desk. With the oncoming *crescendo* he became visible again, rising higher and higher and leaping into the air at that moment when, according to his reckoning, the *forte* should be reached. When the *forte* failed to materialize he looked around in amazement, then stared incredulously at the orchestra, still playing *piano*. He got his bearings with the arrival of the *forte*, and something that he could hear. Fortunately, this comical scene was not repeated at the performance, for the audience would certainly have laughed. Since the hall was filled to overflowing, and the applause most enthusiastic, Beethoven's friends arranged a repetition of the concert, which brought in almost as much money as had the first. Beethoven's financial embarrassment was eased for the moment, but he was to suffer many more, and for the same reasons.

No diminution of Beethoven's creative powers was as

yet noticeable. But from that time onward, as his increasing deafness made it impossible for him to hear any music at all, it was inevitable that this should adversely affect his fantasy. His constant striving to be original and to break new paths was no longer subject to aural control. Is it any wonder that his works became steadily less coherent and less intelligible? There are those, to be sure, who flatter themselves that they understand these late works, and in their enthusiasm, go so far as to label them masterpieces. I am not among them, and confess freely that I have never been able to develop a taste for the later Beethoven. I include among these even the much admired Ninth Symphony, whose first three movements, despite flashes of genius, strike me as inferior to any of the movements of the preceding eight symphonies, and whose fourth movement I consider so monstrous and tasteless and, in its representation of Schiller's Ode, so trivial that I cannot imagine its having been written by a man of Beethoven's genius. I find in it a confirmation of what I noted in Vienna; namely, that Beethoven was wanting in esthetic cultivation and feeling for beauty.

At the time when I made his acquaintance, he had ceased to play either publicly or at private gatherings, and only once did I have occasion to hear him play. This was quite accidentally during a rehearsal of a new Trio in D Major in his apartment. It was no pleasure, firstly, because the piano was out of tune, which bothered Beethoven not at all, since he could not hear it, and, secondly, because little was left of his once celebrated virtuosity. In *forte* passages he hit the keys so hard that the strings rattled, and in *piano*, so softly that whole groups of notes never sounded at all, with the result that it was impossible to follow without the piano score as a guide. I was deeply moved by so tragic a fate. It is bad enough for anyone to be deaf, let alone a musician. Beethoven's constant melancholy was never a mystery to me again.

In the autumn of 1814 the rulers of Europe and their ministers assembled for what was to go down in history as the Congress of Vienna. Great crowds of the curious and the idle converged on Vienna to witness the festival occasions with which, in unprecedented magnificence, the Emperor planned to honor his guests. Several of these affairs had already taken place prior to the Emperor's return, and their brilliance had whetted the public appetite for what was to follow. I took part in one of them. It was an evening musicale in the courtyard of the palace, given either for the Emperor or for Prince Schwarzenberg, I forget which. A platform was set up for the orchestra and the chorus in the middle of the courtyard, which was surrounded by tall buildings. Facing the performers from a balcony were the Court and its retinue. The remaining space below was thronged by the general public. I was shocked when I saw the setting and the crowd, already numbering in the thousands, for I had undertaken to play a concerto, and now feared that I might be unable to make myself heard in this enormous space. It was too late to withdraw, however, and I delivered myself to my fate. It all went better than I had expected. I observed during the playing of the overture that the tall buildings surrounding the courtyard acted as a sounding board, and I stepped out for my own turn with renewed courage. The first tones of my solo relieved me of the fear that the night air might affect the strings unfavorably. My violin had its usual strength and brilliance. The public maintained absolute silence during my playing, and every nuance could be heard plainly. The effect was most favorable, and I was applauded accordingly. I have never played before a more numerous or more receptive audience.

Among the many visitors drawn to Vienna by the congress were a number of artists, who had reckoned this to be a propitious time to present themselves in Vienna. In this they were deceived, for the resident artists were all giving concerts, too, and supply rather exceeded demand, with the inevitable effect on attendance. An exception was the concert given by my wife and myself December 11, which drew a large and brilliant audience. At this concert I introduced the overture to my *Faust*, which was received with great applause. The critic of the *Musikalische Zeitung* wrote, "It increased our desire to hear this opera, which was completed a year ago, in its entirety."

Many art lovers among the ministers and foreign diplomats, who had heard me for the first time at this concert, visited me and expressed the desire to hear me as a quartet player. This prompted me to arrange several musicales during the period of the conference, at which I presented the new compositions I had written for Tost. I still recall with great satisfaction the delight with which these offerings were received. I was supported, to be sure, by the best artists in Vienna, so that, with respect to performance, nothing was left to be desired. I usually began with a quartet, followed with a quintet, and closed with either the Octet or the Nonet.

I was not the only one who organized musicales for the visitors. Among the others, my friend Zizius particularly distinguished himself. All the visiting artists were introduced to him, with the result that his musicales often developed into real competitions between the indigenous virtuosos and the visitors. It was there that I first heard Hummel play his wonderful septet, as well as other compositions he was producing at that time. I was most attracted, however, by his improvising, which remains to this day unmatched by any other artist. I remember with the greatest pleasure one evening in particular when he fairly outdid even himself. The party was on the point of breaking up when a few of the ladies, thinking it still too early, asked Hummel to play some waltzes. Gallant and accommodating as he always was toward the ladies, he seated himself at the piano and played the desired waltzes, at which the young people in the next room began to dance. I and some of the other artists present gathered around the piano, our hats in our hands, and listened. No sooner had Hummel noticed this new audience than he began to improvise freely, holding, however, to the steady waltz rhythm in order not to disturb the dancers. He took the most striking themes and figures from my own compositions and those of others that had been played in the course of the evening's program and wove them into his waltzes, varying them more fancifully with each repetition. Finally he worked them into a fugue, giving full rein to his contrapuntal wizardry, without ever disturbing the pleasure of the dancers. Then he returned to the gallant style and ended with a bravura which was extraordinary even for him, still exploiting the themes he had originally selected, so that the whole extravaganza had the character of a fully rounded composition. The listeners were delighted, and thanked the ladies whose passion for dancing had provided them with such a treat.

In the meantime my position with respect to the *Theater an der Wien* and its owner had undergone some change. With Count Palffy, I had had a serious falling out. The occasion was the following: One evening, as I entered the theater I found Buchwieser, the third conductor, but also father of the prima donna,[15] preparing to conduct in place of Seyfried. I promptly reminded him that I alone was authorized to conduct in Seyfried's absence and requested him to withdraw. This he refused to do, remarking that the Count himself had requested him to conduct, and this at the express wish of his daughter, who preferred to sing under his direction. As all my protests proved to be in vain, and as I considered it beneath my dignity to play violin under so obscure a conductor, I left the orchestra and went home. The next day I complained in writing to the Count about this intrusion upon my contractual prerogatives and demanded that it not be repeated.

[15] Kathinka Buchwieser (1789–1828), a celebrated singer, later member of Schubert's circle of intimates.

Dorette Spohr.

Above. The Ducal Palace in Braunschweig as it appeared when Spohr was a member of the Court Orchestra. It was destroyed by fire during the revolution of 1830. *Below*. The Palace at Gotha as it appeared in Spohr's time.

Instead of responding with the expected apologies, the Count urged on by the prima donna, who, in turn, was annoyed by my refusal to play under her father, replied with insults, which I returned with interest. From that time on the Count and his creatures made things as difficult for me as possible. To make matters worse, Palffy had succeeded in leasing both court theaters, and favored them over his own. He took the best singers and the better part of the chorus and added them to the personnel of the *Kaerntnerthor Theater*, with the result that not much could be given at the *Theater an der Wien* except spectacles and folk operas. As I was not obliged to participate in such productions, there was not much for me to do. It was clear that I would be dropped at the expiration of my contract. Now that Napoleon had been defeated, and all indications were that Europe could expect a period of general peace, I was again anxious to get on with my old project of a European tour. I proposed to the Count that we terminate our contractual relationship at the conclusion of the second year on the condition that he pay me half of my salary for the third. He agreed, and we parted peacefully.

I hastened now to get everything in readiness for a launching of the tour in the spring. My plan was to include Germany, Switzerland, and Italy, with emphasis on the latter, which I longed to visit. I proposed also to take the children along, as I could foresee that their mother would hardly endure so long a separation. This meant a special carriage capable of accommodating both the family and the instruments. It proved difficult to build one light enough to be drawn by three post horses. A satisfactory model was finally designed by Langhans, the ingenious machinist at the *Theater an der Wien*, and built accordingly. Our baggage, including the harp, in a leather case, was carried on the hard top of the carriage, and the violin in a space provided under the coachman's seat, leaving the entire space inside the carriage free for the travelers.

In my relationship to Tost there had also been a serious change. I had recently given him four new manuscripts, the octet, two quartets, and a second quintet, without having received the agreed upon fee. At first I thought nothing of it. Then suddenly there was a spate of rumors that the rich Tost had suffered severe losses and was on the verge of ruin. I began to take these rumors seriously when he failed to appear at a musicale where I was to play some of his manuscripts, contenting himself with merely sending the music. I returned the manuscripts myself, hoping to get at the heart of the matter. I found the usually jovial man in a state of severe depression. He admitted his difficulties without hesitation, adding that he found it particularly painful to be unable to meet his obligations to me. Since his plans for the future would certainly have to be changed, if not dropped altogether, he proposed to return to me all of my manuscripts before expiration of the contracted period, thus freeing me to dispose of them to a publisher. He wished further to compensate me for such losses as I might incur through this change in arrangements, by a note for one hundred ducats, to be honored as soon as his circumstances would

permit. He thereupon gathered together all the manuscripts that I had given him and handed them over to me.
My own feelings were that Tost had amply rewarded
such a brief ownership simply by making it possible for
us to furnish our apartment so cheaply, and I refused
to consider any further settlement. I noted, however,
that this seemed to hurt Tost's pride, and I finally accepted his note, knowing full well that, in view of my
forthcoming tour, there would be no thought of cashing
it for some time to come.

I sold the Tost manuscripts to two Vienna publishers.
Because they had already earned a considerable renown
through their frequent performance, I received respectable sums for them.

At the beginning of 1815 I wrote an additional Quartet in C Major (Opus 29, No. 2) and a new Violin Concerto (Opus 38), plus a set of variations intended for
use on the tour and which remained unpublished. These
last two compositions were included in the program for
my farewell concert on February 15. This concert, my
last in Vienna, was most appreciatively covered by the
Musikalische Zeitung. The verdict on the new concerto
was: "Very difficult, both for soloist and for the accompanying orchestra. A beautiful, superior composition;
lovely, fluent song, surprising modulations, many bold
canonic imitations, novel, charming, and ingenious instrumentation. Especially irresistible is the melting adagio."
And in conclusion: "As to the achievements of this great
artist, there is here and, indeed, in all Germany, one
unanimous opinion. We still remember with the great-

est pleasure his triumph, two years ago, over his rival, Rode. He is now leaving us to set out on an extended tour. His first destination is Prague, where his *Faust* is in preparation. We wish him well! By virtue of his talent and his open, manly bearing, he has erected for himself an enduring monument in our hearts."

I had, indeed, intended to go first to Prague, for the performance of my *Faust*, which had already been prepared by Carl Maria von Weber. But the plan had to be dropped, the reason being that I received from my former intendant, Baron von Reibnitz, in Breslau, a letter inviting me to spend the summer months with his friends, the family of Prince von Carolath, at their summer place, Carolath, in Silesia. It was the Prince's wish that his two daughters, one of whom played harp, the other piano, have lessons from my wife. Everything would be done to make our stay at their charmingly situated palace as agreeable as possible. He, Baron Reibnitz, who had also been invited for the summer, would be endlessly pleased if we could accept the invitation and make it possible for us all to be together again.

Since spring and summer are, in any case, not the best seasons for concerts, and since a stay at Carolath promised much pleasure for Dorette and the children, I accepted. I hastened the preparations for our departure, accordingly, in order to get in some concerts in Breslau and the vicinity before pleasant weather set in. First came the sale of our furniture and house equipment, which went off without difficulty, as a host of buyers presented themselves as soon as the sale was announced. Since our effects were most elegant, and almost new, the buyers outbid one another, with the result that we realized far more than we had had any reason to expect. I took our profits from the sale, as well as my Vienna savings, which were still in paper money, to a banker and exchanged them for gold currency. No sooner had I done so than Vienna was hit by the news of Napoleon's escape from Elba and his landing in France, and the bottom dropped out of the exchange. Had I waited one more day to change my money, I would have suffered a loss of more than fifty ducats.

When I had first conceived the idea of an extended tour through Europe, it occurred to me to take along an album in which I could collect compositions of all the composers who might cross our path. I began immediately with the Viennese, and received from all those composers whom I knew examples from each, handwritten and, in most cases, conceived especially for my album. The most treasurable is one by Beethoven. It is a three-voiced canon to the words from Schiller's *Jungfrau von Orleans: Kurz ist der Schmerz, und ewig die Freude.* It is noteworthy that (1) Beethoven, whose handwriting, either in music or in prose, was usually illegible, must have taken particular care with this entry, for it is immaculate from beginning to end, and this despite the fact that he even had to draw the lines without a ruler; and (2) after the entrance of the third voice, a measure is missing, which I had to supply myself. The entry closes with the words: "Dear Spohr, wherever you go, and wherever you encounter true art and true artists, please remember me, your friend, Ludwig van Beethoven, Vienna, March 3, 1815."

VI

JOURNEY TO SILESIA

(1815)

Following a melancholy leave-taking from our beloved Vienna, where we had experienced such happy times, we set off on our great journey March 8, 1815. My brother Ferdinand, whose contract at the *Theater an der Wien* had another year to run, remained behind. Our first stop was at Bruenn, where we gave a concert. How it went I can no longer remember. My only recollection is that I was most dissatisfied with the orchestral accompaniment. In this connection I had certainly been spoiled by my excellent orchestra in Vienna.

From Bruenn we traveled to Breslau, where we gave two concerts in April, both ill-attended. Everyone was depressed by the renewal of warfare and the sacrifices required for rearmament. A less favorable atmosphere for concert enterprises could hardly be imagined. But in so musical a city, as Breslau had always been, there were, even in wartime, those for whom music was a necessity. I was, therefore, often invited to private musicales, where I could play my Vienna compositions from Tost's briefcase. They were very well received, especially the two quintets, and I had to repeat them frequently.

One beautiful spring evening I arrived with my family in Carolath. Not far from the palace we had had to cross a small stream by ferry, and thus our arrival was not unnoticed. We found the entire princely family assembled at the foot of the steps in the courtyard, and were most cordially welcomed. The Prince himself led us to our quarters. After we had changed, we were summoned to supper. The Prince, a rather ceremonious but otherwise friendly and benevolent man of fifty-eight or sixty years, received us at the entrance to the dining room and introduced us to the assembled company. There were the Princess, his second wife, her sister, an enthusiast for poetry and music, his two daughters by his first marriage, lovely girls of fifteen and seventeen, and their tutor, Herr Kartscher, a highly cultivated young man. The conversation at table, aside from the rather old-fashioned formality of the Prince, was relaxed and animated, and demonstrated to me that we were in a cultivated group, susceptible to everything beautiful.

Next day began the routine which, with few exceptions, was to endure for the length of our stay. In the mornings, Dorette instructed the Princesses, the older on harp, the younger on piano, while I began the musical instruction of our children. The latter were then permitted to attend the lessons given the Princesses by their tutor, who was kind enough to adapt his instruction, insofar as possible, to their (my childrens') capacities. During this time my wife and I occupied ourselves with our own musical studies, or I composed. Since the princely family was very fond of song, I took advantage of the opportunity to write two volumes of *Lieder* to texts provided by the Princess' sister from her collection of poetry. These *Lieder* were published by Peters as Opus 37 and Opus 41.

When the work and study of the forenoon were finished, we changed for the noonday meal, as the princely family always appeared *en parure*. The remainder of the day was devoted to sociability and pleasure. When the weather was fine we took coffee in the palace garden, and towards evening there would be an excursion by carriage in the surrounding countryside. A frequent destination was a dairy which belonged to the Prince, where we would have a rural supper. If the weather was bad, or if there were visitors, we would have music in the palace. At the outset the musical offerings were such as my wife and I could provide on violin, harp, and piano. After Reibnitz's arrival, we tried quartets. The Prince's old valet, who had played cello in his youth, had to produce his instrument. The village schoolmaster played viola, and Reibnitz, second violin. Unfortunately, I had no quartets with me other than my own, which had hardly been written for such players. Thus, our first attempt was very discouraging. Since the others were both enthusiastic and industrious, and wanting neither in pa-

tience nor in endurance, we managed, after many rehearsals, to make a presentable go of it with two of my quartets. Our listeners were not too spoiled in the way of
artistic pleasures, and rewarded our endeavors with great
applause. A polonaise that I composed at that time (Opus
40) was also much liked, and was often requested at our
gatherings, perhaps only because the participants and the
listeners had been in at the birth, so to speak.

When my family and I had passed the first two months
in this uniform but nevertheless agreeable way at Carolath, the Prince informed us one day at noon, rather
solemnly, that he would be obliged to leave his guests
for a day. It was his custom each year to journey to
Glogau on June 24 for the celebration of the Feast of
St. John by the Freemasons. This prompted me, after
we had left the table, to identify myself to our host as a
Freemason. The Prince was most agreebly surprised,
and promptly invited me to accompany him. I have forgotten to mention that I became a Freemason in the second degree after my first year in Gotha. A year later,
in Berlin I received the third and master's degree. Since
Freemasonry was forbidden in Vienna, I had not attended a lodge meeting for three and a half years, and
was now most anxious once again to attend a gathering
of brothers. Thus the Prince's invitation to accompany
him to Glogau was more than welcome.

The preparations were appropriately brilliant. The
great carriage with the princely coat-of-arms was pulled
out of the coach house and dusted off, a hunter and another servant were attired in festive livree, and the Prince,

himself, appeared for the first time in his state uniform with the star upon his breast. We started off early in the morning of the twenty-fourth. At the lodge rooms, the Prince and his guest were welcomed by a deputation. After the business meeting came a banquet at which I joined the musical lodge members, led their singing, and offered on my own account, in a booming bass, a number of Mason songs, as well as *In diesen heiligen Hallen* from *The Magic Flute*. Among the musician members I met a number of friends from my earlier tour of Silesia, all of whom were at special pains to honor me with attention. Indeed, the master of the lodge, himself, welcomed the "famous artist" to the company and thanked the Prince for having introduced him. The Prince appeared very happy in the reflected glory of his guest, for thereafter he redoubled his attentions to me and my family, which even previously had often been such as to occasion us some embarrassment.

After another six to eight most agreeable weeks, we continued our journey via Dresden and Leipzig to Gotha. Dorette was so happy to be at home again after an absence of almost three years that I could not bring myself to set off again without a suitable interval. We settled down for a few months and I confined my traveling to some minor excursions in the immediate area.

INTERVAL

In the fall of 1815, Spohr participated in the third Thuringian Festival at Frankenhausen, and shortly afterwards he and his wife set out on the long journey that was to take them to Switzerland and across the Alps into Italy. At Frankenhausen he began a diary which he kept up throughout the trip, and it is the diary text that we follow from here until the end of the journey.

VII

JOURNEY TO SWITZERLAND
AND ITALY

(1815–17)

FOLLOWING AN INTERVAL OF THREE YEARS, the artists of
Thuringia have assembled here again to celebrate the
liberation of Germany on the anniversary of the Battle
of Leipzig. Today, the first day of the festival, was devoted to my cantata, *Das befreite Deutschland,* and
Gottfried Weber's *Te Deum.* Since it hardly becomes
me as a composer to pass judgment on my own work, I
shall speak here only of the performance.

The soloists were not uniformly good, and the arias
and ensembles, consequently, were the least effective.
The chorus and orchestra, on the other hand, were excellent, and the overture and all the big choruses, accordingly, succeeded splendidly. Most popular were the
double chorus of the Fleeing French and the Pursuing
Russians, the subsequent Prayer of Thanksgiving of the

German people, and the concluding chorus and fugue. Again I had occasion to observe that, in large auditoriums and with a large orchestra and chorus, the simplest numbers have the greatest effect, assuming a noble and dignified style of composition, whereas a richly figured scoring and rapid harmonic progressions are out of place.

Frankenhausen, October 20, 1815

There was a concert of mixed content in the following order:

Mozart's Symphony in C Major, precisely and spiritedly played and irresistibly effective! (This performance convinced me that, in this setting and with adequate orchestral forces, the four themes of the concluding fugue, where they come together at the end, can be followed easily by a practiced ear. Whereas this passage had formerly impressed me as simply a technical tour de force, I recognized this impression today as an error.)

My own Concerto in E minor. (I noted again that virtuosity appeals to a large public far more than the art of composition. Everyone was delighted with my playing, but very few took any notice of the composition.)

Italian aria with Chorus by Paer. (This aria from the oratorio *La Religione* is written in so unchurchly a style that it could, with a different text, be transplanted into an opera buffa.)

My own Adagio and Potpourri for Clarinet.

And, finally, a patriotic chorus to the tune of "God Save the King," with orchestral and organ accompaniment by Methfessel. The audience, to whom copies of the text had been distributed, joined in.

Poor Bischoff came off badly at this third Frankenhausen Festival. The reason for the deficit was the billeting of Russian troops in the area, which hindered the attendance of both the urban and rural inhabitants. As Bischoff was in no position to cover the deficit from his own resources, the assembled artists, at my suggestion, agreed to assume their own travel expenses and to cover them by concerts given in their home towns. (I gave mine at Gotha, assisted by Andreas Romberg, who had now been concertmaster there for two years.)

Nuremberg, November 16, 1815

Music seems to be little cultivated here, for the orchestra is conspicuously bad. There was, to be sure, no shortage either of listeners or applause at our concert yesterday, but the orchestra spoiled everything that it accompanied.

Munich, December 12, 1815

Our stay here has been rich in artistic pleasures. On the very day of our arrival we heard an interesting concert, the first of the twelve Winter Concerts given each year by the Royal Orchestra for its own benefit. These concerts are well attended, and most deservedly so. The orchestra has twelve first and twelve second violins, eight violas, ten cellos, and six double basses. Violins and basses are excellent, as are also the wind instruments, with the possible exception of the horns. Each concert includes an entire symphony (a practice the more to be praised, as it is growing less and less common and the public is losing its feeling for this noblest of all instrumental forms), then an overture, and two vocal and two instrumental solos. Since the Munich Orchestra still enjoys a reputation as one of the best in the world, my expectations were high, and I hasten to record that in the performance of Beethoven's Symphony in C minor, which opened the concert, they were unsurpassed. It is hardly possible that this symphony could be played with more fire and more strength and, at the same time, with more tenderness and with more precise attention to every nuance. It had, accordingly, a greater effect than I would have thought possible, although I had heard it frequently in Vienna and under the composer's direction. Even so, I found no reason to reverse my earlier judgment. It has many individual beauties, but they do not add up to a classical whole. The very first theme, in particular, lacks the dignity essential to the opening of a symphony. This aside, however, the short, easily grasped theme lends itself well to thematic elaboration, and the composer has combined it most imaginatively and effectively with the other principal motives of the first movement. The adagio, in A flat, is very beautiful in part, but the same progressions and modulations are repeated too often, despite the ever richer figuration. The scherzo is highly original, and of genuinely romantic texture, but the trio, with its tumbling bass runs, is too baroque for my taste. The last movement, with its empty noise, is the least satisfactory, although the return of the scherzo is such a happy idea that one can only envy the composer who could have thought of such a thing. It is quite irresistible. What a pity that the effect is so soon dissipated by the resumption of the noise.

In the first concert we also heard Rovelli,[1] a young violinist, only recently engaged, who played a Concerto in C minor by Lafont[2] most excellently. This young artist, a pupil of Kreutzer, combines with the virtues of the Parisian school that which is so often lacking among its products; namely, feeling and individual taste. The virtue of this school is the careful cultivation of technic, often to the neglect of artistry. This is not the case with Rovelli, for he is a good sight reader, and as I later had occasion to learn in the performance of my own quartets, a good accompanist.

On December 3 we played for the King and Queen in the presence of a few chosen members of the court. Both monarchs seemed to take great interest in our playing, for they overwhelmed us with kindness. In addition to us, a Madame Dulcken, an excellent virtuoso, played, with her daughter and pupil, a rondo for two pianos by Steibelt.[3]

[1] Pietro Rovelli (1793–1838), Italian violinist from Bergamo, who had great successes at that time in Munich and later in Vienna.

[2] Philippe Lafont (1781–1839), a celebrated French violin virtuoso, pupil both of Rodolphe Kreutzer and of Rode, whom he succeeded as solo violinist to the Emperor of Russia in 1808. In 1815 he returned to Paris and was appointed solo violinist to Louis XVIII.

[3] Daniel Steibelt (1765–1823), German pianist and composer, so celebrated in his time, according to Grove, that he was regarded by many as a rival to Beethoven. He was principally active in London and Paris

On the sixth was our public concert in the *Redou-tensaal*, which the Queen honored with her presence, a distinction accorded no other artist in recent years. It was a great pleasure for me to hear my own compositions played so well again.

Wuerzburg, December 26, 1815

On the way from Munich we gave, on the wing, so to speak, four concerts in four different cities in ten days. All had been arranged in advance. The concerts were well attended, and brought in a good deal of money. We played in Nuremberg on the sixteenth, in Erlangen on the eighteenth, in Bamberg on the twenty-second and yesterday here. It has been very strenuous, especially for Dorette, what with the continual packing and unpacking, rehearsals, and concerts.

Frankfurt/Main, January 14, 1816

Our visit here has been dismal. Apart from our own, not a single concert the whole time, not even a private musicale! When we were here eight years ago, we hardly found time to accommodate all those who wished us to participate in musicales. Today it hardly occurs to a Frankfurt music lover (if there is such a thing!) to avail himself of our talents.

Darmstadt, February 9, 1816

Forced by Dorette's illness to spend almost a month here, I have had ample time to acquaint myself with the

---

until he succeeded Boieldieu as director of the French Opera at St. Petersburg in 1810.

condition of music in Darmstadt. Not that much good can be said of it. The Grand Duke[4] loves music and spends a lot of money on it; but he is one-sided, egotistical, and restricts himself to music for the theater. His great passion is to combine in his own person the roles of both musical director and régisseur at the opera rehearsals. Since he regards himself as infallible in both capacities, and permits the slightest interference with his directions neither from the actual musical director nor from the *régisseur*, things have a tendency to go wrong. As a musical director he may well be the best of all the Grand Dukes—which is not to say, necessarily, that he is a good one! This is clear enough just from his selection of works for his theater. The latter is so generously financed that no notice need be taken of public taste in the selection of repertoire, and it would be quite possible to offer only the best. The Grand Duke, however, chooses the repertoire himself, with the result that not only is the mediocre favored but also the very good is excluded, the Cherubini operas, for example, which the Grand Duke cannot abide. He permitted the latter's *Der Wassertraeger (Les Deux Journeés)*, to be sure, but only the first act. Nor do Mozart's operas meet with his approval. *Don Giovanni* came up a few days ago, following rehearsals on thirty successive nights of Poissl's[5] *Athalie*. After the orchestra, liberated from the deadly

[4] Grand Duke Ludwig I of Hesse (1753-1830), another of the pioneers of conducting with baton.

[5] Johann Nepomuk Freiherr von Poissl (1783-1865), for many years general manager of the Court Opera in Munich and one of the early composers of indigenous German opera.

boredom of *Athalie*, had brought the first act to a jubilant conclusion, the Grand Duke turned to the musical director and said, "After Poissl, I can find no pleasure in Mozart!"

With the generous salaries prevailing, the soloists could be a lot better than they are. It is said that the Grand Duke prefers mediocrities, who are more amenable to his direction. The chorus (thirty men and thirty women) is excellent. The orchestra is large, and includes a number of good artists along with many of mediocre ability. No orchestra in the world has a harder lot, for every musician must spend every evening from six o'clock until nine or ten in the theater. There is an opera every Sunday. Two other days, there is theater. The four remaining days are devoted to the Grand Duke's opera rehearsals. Only the Grand Duke's illness can prevent them. When this is the case, no opera is given. Not long ago, the Grand Duke was confined to his room for several weeks because of some injury to his leg. During this period there were neither rehearsals nor performances. He wished to indicate, apparently, that without his guiding hand, nothing could be prepared.

It is quite a sight to see this proud, already rather rheumatic old man, in uniform, with the star on his breast, standing behind the desk, giving the beat, directing the chorus and supers, yelling *"piano"* or *"forte"* to the orchestra. If he knew what it was all about, he would be the best of all possible opera directors, for he has not only enthusiasm and endurance, but also the full authority accruing to a Grand Duke. Unfortunately, his knowledge of a score does not extend beyond the first violin part. He once played violin in his youth, and never lets the violinists forget it. As for all the rest, the singers can sing out of tune, the wind instruments can come in a measure too soon or too late—he doesn't notice a thing.

As the Grand Duke refused to make his orchestra available to us for a public concert (his answer to my entreaty was that he could not spare an orchestra from the theater for even one single evening), we were about to leave town without having played there when the casino offered us a one-night engagement. We accepted. Dorette and I played a sonata and two concerto movements with piano accompaniment. Dorette closed with the Fantasie in C minor. The violinists of the orchestra, who would have liked to hear me, and Backofen, my wife's former teacher, were not permitted to attend. At his rehearsal the night before in his theater, the Grand Duke had said, "Let no one be missing tomorrow night!"

Strasbourg, March 6, 1816

Among the most devoted music lovers is the lawyer Lobenstein, director of a well-established amateur music society. Their strongly constituted orchestra consists mostly of amateurs, and they do quite well with pieces that are not too difficult and which they have rehearsed sufficiently. According to a law held over from the time of the Revolution, anyone giving a concert in France, who advertizes his concert and charges a price of admission, must turn over one-fifth of his receipts to the directorate of the local theater. In order to help me circumvent this law, Lobenstein proposed that I play in his hall, and on the day set for one of his concerts. The concert was announced only by word of mouth, but, even so, it was so well-attended that more than one hundred persons had to be turned away from the sizable hall. The attendance, plus the enthusiastic applause, prompted me to give a second public concert, for which I arranged a fixed-fee settlement with the theater directorate. The orchestra was the same on both occasions, made up partly of amateurs, partly of professionals. The strings were rather good; the winds, for the most part, weak. As the latter are much employed in my compositions, there was a good deal of mischief. My quartets and quintets, on the other hand, which I played frequently in private musicales, were well-accompanied. Although the Strasbourgers are rather behind the inhabitants of the larger German cities in musical cultivation, and know little of our newest music and its nature, my compositions seemed to appeal to them. As a result of my stay here my compositions, previously hardly known, are now in demand and are being stocked by the music dealers.

Muenster bei Colmar, March 26, 1816

For the past fortnight we have been here in this little factory town in the Vosges, visiting a rich manufacturer named Jacques Hartmann. Our host, a passionate music lover, had been advised by musical director Brandt, of Karlsruhe, that we would be passing through Colmar. From Strasbourg he had ascertained the exact day on which we would be passing through. He blocked our way and, with friendly persuasion, induced us to follow him to Colmar. Arriving there at dusk, we were welcomed most cordially by his family and promptly conducted through the garden to a brilliantly illuminated concert hall, decorated with the names of our great composers, among whom—probably as of that very morning—my own was accorded a modest place. Hartmann's orchestra was already assembled, and greeted us with an overture, by no means badly executed. The orchestra is composed of members of Hartmann's family and employees of his textile factory. Insofar as possible, apparently, he employs only those who are musically gifted, and thus he has been able to assemble a full orchestra which, with sufficient rehearsal, is capable of playing pieces that are not too difficult. Hartmann, himself, is a bassoon virtuoso, and has a lovely tone and considerable dexterity. His sister and his daughter play piano. The latter, a child of eight years, is the jewel of this amateur orchestra. She plays very difficult compositions with admirable finesse and precision. Even more astonishing to me was her extraordinarily musical ear. At some distance from the piano, she could distinguish and identify the notes of the most complicated and dissonant sounds. . . . After the family had played their pieces we, in our turn, offered one of our duets, and found a most grateful and enthusiastic reception. . . .

Three days ago we gave a very well-attended concert in Colmar, arranged by Hartmann through his musical friends there. Since the orchestra, consisting almost wholly of amateurs, was very bad, I thought it best to forego my own compositions and confined myself to easier pieces by Rode and Kreutzer. Following the sonata which my wife and I played, a wreath was thrown from a box bearing the following inscription:

Couple savant dans l'art heureux
Qui fit placer au rang des Dieux
L'antique chantre de la Grèce
D'un instrument mélodieux
Et de la harpe enchanteresse,
Dont accords délicieux
Nous causent une double ivresse.
Faul-il, que les tristes apprêts
D'un départ qui nous désespère,
Mêlent d'inutiles regrets
Aux charmes que votre art opère?
Ah! près de nous il faut rester!
Quelle raison pour s'en défendre?
A nos voeux, si Spohr veut se rendre,
Il pourra, j'ose l'attester,
Se lasser de nous enchanter,
Jamais nous lasser de l'entendre.

Par E. C. Couteret, habitant de Colmar.

Basel, April 2, 1816

Herr Tollmann,[6] a good violinist and director, and the friendliest and most obliging man I ever met, had, with the help of the local *Musikverein*, prepared everything for our concert. All that remained was to obtain the Mayor's

[6] Johann Michael Tollmann (1777–1829).

approval to raise the admission price a half laubthaler. This was promptly granted. Tollmann conducted me to the directors of the *Musikverein*, who proved to be both engaging and cultivated. Certainly they contradicted in a trice the rumor current in Alsace, according to which the Baslers are cold and discourteous and ill disposed toward visitors. I was received by all whom I visited with courtesy and even with deference. As the orchestra, with the exception of four or five professionals, is composed of amateurs, the accompaniments for my solo pieces, particularly on the part of the winds, were horrible. How one must pity poor Tollmann, who has to hear such music year in and year out! And yet, according to his own testimony, the orchestras in the other Swiss cities are even worse. If that is so, then the state of music in Switzerland is even more miserable than in Alsace. The good people here find pleasure in compositions which we in Germany found intolerable even in Pleyel's time. Of Mozart, Haydn, and Beethoven, they barely know the names. But still, they love music, and the best part of it is—they are easy to please. As bad as the orchestral movements were in our concert, the people were satisfied, and insisted that on this occasion the orchestra had fairly distinguished itself. . . .

Zuerich, April 10, 1816

Here, too, there is a *Musikverein*. These *Vereine* in the Swiss cities are a great blessing for the traveling musician, for they take over the arrangements for a concert most obligingly. Ours took place on the fourth day following our arrival. Aside from playing, we had nothing further to do. The accompaniment was, to be sure, again very bad, and I suffered the more for having let myself be persuaded to play a concert of my own compositions. At the rehearsal, thanks to countless repetition of the more difficult passages, I managed to make it sound something like music; but at the concert the orchestra was in such a state of consternation that it all went to pieces again. Fortunately, the audience appeared to notice nothing wrong, and expressed great satisfaction with everything. The receipts were even more gratifying than they had been in Basel.

Bern, April 20, 1816

A most agreeable journey with lovely weather! From a modest hill, about an hour's drive from here, we saw for the first time the splendid chain of the Alps in all their majesty. We greeted them jubilantly! And now we are impatient to come closer!

The Bern *Musikgesellschaft* obligingly took over the arrangements for our concert and relieved me of all the administrative details. Attendance was greater than that ever previously accorded a visiting artist, but the receipts, because of the lower admission price, less than in Zuerich. The orchestra was, if possible, even worse than those in Zuerich and Basel, and the audience even less sophisticated, with very few exceptions. The conductor is a brother of Carl Maria von Weber,[7] and it is said that he is an excellent theoretician. As violinist and conductor he is very weak.

[7] Edmund Weber (1766–1828), Carl Maria von Weber's half-brother.

As the season is too far advanced to concertize in the other Swiss cities, we shall interrupt our journey for the time being and settle down in some pleasant spot in the Bernese Oberland for the rest which Dorette so desperately needs for the restoration of her health. Our acquaintances here recommended a village near Thun. We drove there yesterday and found everything made to order for us. The village is called Thierachern, and is situated on the most beautiful spot on earth that I have yet seen. We rented two rooms in a local hostelry, and are now joyously anticipating the pleasures of a bucolic existence. I plan to spend my time on some violin compositions with easy orchestral accompaniment, as I am told that the Italian orchestras are even worse than those of the French provinces. . . .

Thierachern, May 16, 1816

We have begun to apportion our time between work and play. In the mornings, while I compose, Dorette gives the children lessons in writing, arithmetic, geography, etc.; in the afternoons, I give instruction in piano and singing. Then we go off into the countryside. If the weather is such as to permit a longer excursion, we take a frugal supper in some country inn or at a dairy, and return, often late in the evening. If the weather is variable we go into Thun, armed with umbrellas, look in at the post office for letters from home, borrow books at the library against rainy days, and do our shopping. This daily moving about in the wonderful, pure, balmy air strengthens our bodies, refreshes our spirits, and makes us happy and glad. Under such circumstances work goes rapidly and easily. I have already finished a Concerto for Violin in the form of a vocal *scena*[8] and a Duet for Two Violins. . . .

I have observed something here that interests me greatly as a musician. The handy man of the house and some of the girls from the neighborhood give a little serenade before our window every Sunday evening. They intone their songs in the manner common to wind instruments when not adjusted by a helping hand; i. e., the thirds are a bit sharp, the fourths rather sharper, and the diminished sevenths appreciably flat. In truth, this is the intonation native to the human ear unattuned to our tempered scale. To these untutored singers our scale would sound fully as false as theirs does to us. It is noteworthy and almost disturbing that we have had to compromise the natural scale in order to achieve our present harmonic wealth. For without our tempered system we would be restricted to adjacent tonalities and denied the enharmonic changes which constitute the *haut goût* of modern harmony. And yet it seems to me that this very deviation from nature has made it possible for music to develop as an art, while other arts have had to be content with copying nature, or at least with accepting nature as a point of departure. The songs of these untutored singers have quite an individual flavor, and when I have acquainted myself with the local dialect, which is very similar to the Allemanic, I shall try to copy some of them down. . . .

[8] More properly *scena ed aria*. It is generally referred to in the German translation, *Gesangsszene,* and is the best known of Spohr's violin concertos.

138

Thierachern, August 12

We have just returned from Fribourg, where we attended the Swiss Music Festival. Herr Naegeli, president of the Swiss *Musikgesellschaft*, had invited us during our visit to Zuerich, and had even offered me the directorship, which I accepted. He had forgotten, however, or did not know, that the statutes of the society expressly forbid the employment of a foreigner, or of any nonmember, as director. I declined a subsequent invitation to participate as violinist, as word of the original proposal that I assume the directorship had gotten around, and I did not wish to appear in an inferior capacity. I agreed, however, that we would attend as listeners.

We drove over on June 6, in fine weather. Despite my refusal to participate, we were put up in a private house and provided with tickets to all performances and rehearsals, as well as to a *bal paré*. We were also provided with texts of Haydn's *The Creation* in both French and German. I was further invited to attend the meetings of the society.

Next morning, when I appeared at the meeting, I was greeted with applause and the president announced that I had been unanimously elected an honorary member. He added many flattering comments, and referred most respectfully to our festivals in Frankenhausen. I expressed my thanks, and took the place set aside for me.

The performance of *The Creation* took place that afternoon at three o'clock. The auditorium was satisfactory, and the orchestra well placed, the only disadvantage being that the organ, situated at the opposite end, could not be used. Whereas at former festivals the participants had numbered at least three hundred, there were hardly two hundred on this occasion, and since more than half were in the chorus, the orchestra, particularly in the big choral episodes, was much too weak. Indeed, it was at times inaudible. It was also very bad. The intonation of the strings was insupportable, and the winds, particularly the horns and trumpets, produced sounds from time to time that prompted general laughter. Tollmann conducted with resolution and circumspection, but chose many wrong tempi, taking the arias too slow and the choruses too fast. The chorus was well trained, and sang strongly and cleanly. It consisted almost exclusively of German-Swiss. Among the soloists, however, were two French-Swiss. They sang in their mother tongue, with some comical consequences, especially in the duet between Adam and Eve, where Eve responded to the endearments of her German Adam in French. All this was accepted as a matter of course by the listeners and not surprisingly, since Fribourg is situated on a language border. French is spoken on one side of the Saane, German on the other. The large audience accepted the music undemonstratively. Of the enthusiasm which had so inspired us all at Frankenhausen, there was not a trace.

The rehearsal for the concert took place on the ninth. It had originally been intended that the concert be given in a smaller hall, but when it became apparent that this hall would be too small for the anticipated audience, the plan was abandoned. The larger auditorium meant, of course, or should have meant, a larger orchestra, but there were no parts for the extra instruments. The result was an orchestra considerably weaker than that which had supported *The Creation*, and its deficiencies were even more painfully apparent. But how could it have been otherwise with an orchestra made up of amateurs, and Swiss amateurs at that! The easiest movements had to be repeated six or eight times before they went even tolerably. I admired the patience of the good Tollmann, although compelled to admit that he was predestined for the fate of a conductor of an amateur Swiss orchestra.

At three in the afternoon the remarkable concert began, in an ear-splitting fashion, with the Overture to Gluck's *Iphigenie*. The trumpets were tuned a quarter tone too high, and were blown without regard for the meager strength of the orchestra. If the overture had lasted even a few minutes longer, a good part of the audience would have fled. There followed a succession of amateurs, some singers, some instrumentalists, each with his solo offering. Some of them were quite good. I was particularly impressed with a man from Yverdon, who played a harp concerto by Boscha[9] with taste and precision. Another man whose name I forget—indeed, as I have forgotten them all, as no programs were provided—played a clarinet resembling, in form and tone, a *corno di bassetto*.

We spared ourselves the second half of the program. We were told, however, that a preacher from Lucerne had distinguished himself in a flute concerto, and Tollmann, himself, in a rondo for violin. Unfortunately, we

---

[9] Robert Nikolas Boscha (1789–1856), famous French harpist and composer.

had not known that Tollman would play, or we would have stayed until the end.

Such was the accomplishment of the Swiss *Musikverein*, so famous in Germany! Concertmaster Konradin Kreutzer,[10] from Stuttgart, and his wife, a native of Zuerich, whose acquaintance we had made here, sat next to us at the performances, and we enjoyed exchanging opinions with them. We had to be careful, however, about our facial expressions, as we were continually observed by other listeners, anxious to read in our faces our reactions to what was being offered. Afterwards when we were asked for our verdicts, which happened often, and with a deal of national pride, we chose a middle course between truth and flattery and managed to avoid giving offense.

Journey to Milan, 1816

On September 2, we began our journey. About one o'clock we reached Kandersteg, where I ordered four horses and as many drivers to get us over the Gemmi Pass. The climb lasted a good three and one-half hours, followed by a level stretch around the Gemmihorn and a further climb beginning about a quarter of an hour before Schwaribach. The weather had been pleasant thus far, but we were now met by a hailstorm which soon turned to rain and soaked us through. As it was also getting late, and the most difficult part of the journey still lay ahead, our drivers had no difficulty persuading us to spend the

[10] Konradin Kreutzer (1780–1849), German opera composer and conductor, for many years principal conductor at the *Kaerntnerthor Theater* in Vienna. His most famous opera, *Das Nachtlager in Granada*, is still not entirely forgotten in Germany.

night in Schwaribach. This is, to be sure, only a rough blockhouse, and has nothing in common with hotels of the Swiss valleys, except the overcharging. Since one of the two inhabitable rooms was made available to us and it contained a bed for Dorette and the children and clean straw for the men, we passed the night quite tolerably.

Snow fell during the night, and the morning was bitterly cold. I sent three of the horses back, and had Dorette and the children join us on foot, since the descent to the Leukerbad can not be accomplished on horseback. All vegetation ceased at Schwaribach, including even the beautiful alpine rose. We had a further steep climb to the Staubensee, which was half-covered with ice, and then proceeded for one-half hour through a desolate valley to the final ascent. This climb, leading over fields of snow and ice, was the most difficult stretch of all. Arriving at the top, we were vouchsafed only an instant's glimpse of the abyss opening at our feet before a heavy fog set in. We could only blindly follow our pack horse and its driver, each of us holding on to the person in front of him. The path was incredibly steep, sometimes between vertical rock walls out of which a small path had been blasted. Where the path turned, our horse's head and neck would hang out over the abyss, and the driver had to haul with might and main on a rope fastened to the load, sometimes even haul on his tail, in order to maintain control and prevent his tumbling over. The view below, which we were spared by the fog, is so dizzying at this point, that many sick persons, on their way to the Leuker baths, have not the courage to make the descent, and go back and around by way of Bern, Fribourg, Lausanne, and the Rhone Valley.

After an hour's descent, with no other vegetation than an occasional violet in a cleft in the rocks, we suddenly arrived in a region where the fog lifted and were vouchsafed a stunning view of Leukerbad, still far below. Here we rested a while, recovering our strength after the strenuous descent. Still, many more stops were required before we reached Leukerbad, about eleven o'clock. Only the children seemed to experience no fatigue. They were always out ahead of us.

On Tuesday, the fourth, we continued our journey by carriage to Brig, where we arrived at noon. Here begins Napoleon's famous Simplon Road, a stupendous accomplishment which can hardly be sufficiently admired. We traveled by carriage towards Domo d'Ossola, spending the night in the village of Simpelm. Wednesday, September 5, 1816, was the day on which my lifelong dream was fulfilled, and I beheld with my own eyes the land *"wo die Zitronen bluehen."* After a two-hour descent we reached the Lombardian border and found ourselves suddenly transplanted to the south. We saw forests of chestnut trees, gardens with figs and almonds, and lovely vineyards. With every step the air grew warmer. This was at first most welcome, but became burdensome as the day advanced. We reached Domo d'Ossola by noon, a small, pleasant town, where, for the first time, we were cheated about the price in advance. That afternoon we continued on to Laveno, hard on the shore of beautiful *Lago di Maggiore*, opposite the famous Borromeo Islands. Here we agreed in advance on the price of the night's lodging, only to learn later that we had paid too much by half. Next day we visited the islands, continuing on by the same boat to Sesto Calende at the lower end of the lake. Here we found Italian filth in all its perfection, and oil cooking, so offensive to German palates. On the seventh, we drove to Milan with a Milanese coachman and put up at the *Pensione Suizzera*, which had been recommended to us because of its German cleanliness.

Milan, September 9, 1816

Last night we visited the *Teatro alla Scala*, where they gave *La Statua di Bronza*, an *opera semi-seria* by Solíva, a young composer, recently a pupil at the local conservatory. The size and beauty of the house surprised us. Next to the *San Carlo* in Naples, it is the largest in Italy. It has a commodious parterre, and six rows of boxes, but, because the builders were rather wasteful of space, the theater seats only three thousand people. The price of admission is the same for all seats. The orchestra is very large, with twenty-four violins, eight cellos, and as many basses, plus all the familiar wind instruments, trombones, bass horn, and Turkish music. Still, it is none too large for the auditorium.

The performance surpassed my expectations. It was clean, strong, and secure. Rolla,[11] an artist already known beyond the borders of Italy as a composer, conducted

---

[11] Allessandro Rolla (1757–1841), composer and virtuoso on both violin and viola. Before settling in Milan he was the leader of the orchestra at Parma (1782–1802), where Paganini was among his pupils.

from his post as leader of the violins. There was no further direction, either from piano or time beater, except for a prompter who occasionally beat time for the chorus. The opera itself is more to the German than to the Italian taste, and indicates very plainly that the young composer had chosen German masters, Mozart particularly, rather than Italians as his models. The orchestral part is not so subordinated as is customary in Italian operas, but is rather prominent, sometimes even more so than is good for the song. It is the more surprising that this opera should have met with such approval, since the style itself is still not much in favor. It is not, to be sure, the well worked-out ensembles and finale that have made its fortune, but rather a few insignificant arias, which the singers managed quite well. These were also the only items which were accorded any attention. During the imposing overture and a number of highly expressive accompanied recitatives, the noise in the house was such that one could hardly hear the music. There was card playing in most of the boxes, and loud conversation everywhere. For a stranger anxious to listen attentively, nothing more insupportable can be imagined than this infamous din. Attention is hardly to be expected, however, of people who may have heard the same opera thirty or forty times, and whose purpose in attending is exclusively social, and it is remarkable that they listen even to a few numbers. At the same time, I can imagine nothing more thankless than to write for such a public, and I am astonished that good composers still do it.

After the first act of the opera came a large, serious ballet, distinguished by the skill of a number of dancers and by the splendor of the costumes and decorations. It lasted nearly an hour, so that the first act of the opera had been fairly forgotten. After the second act there was another ballet, comic and considerably shorter. The whole performance listed from eight o'clock until midnight. What hard work for the poor musicians!

September 14, 1816

Last evening we heard a concert given by Ferlendis, a *professore di oboe* from Venice. He played a concerto of his own. Both the concerto and his performance of it were equally appalling, I can imagine no greater tastelessness. In Germany he would certainly have been hooted from the hall. In the second half, Luigi Belloli[12] played a horn concerto, also of his own composition. The piece was hardly better than mediocre, but it was beautifully played. Belloli has a lovely tone, much facility, and a cultivated taste. We left after his number, lest the pleasant impression be obliterated by further exposure to the abominable oboe.

September 16, 1816

This afternoon we attended a concert by the *Societa del Giardino*. Soloists were the Signore Marcolini and Fabré. The former is an alto, very famous in Italy. She has a beautiful voice and much agility, but sings consistently a bit flat. Signora Fabré, the prima donna of *La Scala*, has an exceptionally beautiful voice and a cultivated interpretative style. Although the two singers were about

[12] Luigi Belloli (1770–1817), horn virtuoso and author of a manual on horn playing.

147

equal in voice and artistry, the soprano carried the day, as a violin inevitably will carry the day against a viola. They sang duets and arias by Rossini, Paccini,[13] Bonfichi, and Paer. Everything was done in the same manner, and adorned with the same familiar ornaments, regardless of whether the music was comical or serious. The compositions were almost all consistently dull and wanting in substance, and the performance was frequently disturbed by meaningless figuration in the accompanying orchestra.

September 22, 1816

I dropped in today at a kind of study-concert, where the local amateurs, under the direction of Rolla, play symphonies, especially those of German masters. The string players are mostly amateurs, while the winds are from the orchestra of *La Scala*. They had already played the old Symphony in D by Mozart and some Italian overtures, and were setting to work on Haydn's great Symphony in B flat. The playing was tolerably precise, but without *piano* and *forte* and, on the whole, rather rough. The enterprise, the only one of its kind in Italy, is most praiseworthy, since it affords the local music lovers an opportunity to become acquainted with our wonderful instrumental compositions. If I am not mistaken, these weekly study-concerts take place in the home of a Signor Motto, who is also the possessor of a notable collection of fine violins.

Indeed, there are many fine instruments here. A Signor Caroli has two very beautiful Stradivari.[14] Rolla also has

[13] Presumably Giovanni Pacini (1796–1867), the composer of some

a lovely one. A Count Gozio de Solence has a large collection of violins, including instruments by Amati, Guarneri, and Guadagnini, not to mention four Stradivari that have never been played upon. Two of the instruments date from the year of Stradivarius' death, in other words, from 1737, when he was an old man of ninety-three. The date shows in the instruments, whose finish betrays the trembling hands of a tottering old man. The two others are from his prime, and are very beautiful. The tone is full and strong, although a bit new and wooden. In order to come fully into their own they would have to be played for at least ten years.

September 28, 1816

Last night was our concert at *La Scala*. The orchestra was seated as usual. Dorette and I and our vocal soloist took our places under the proscenium, before the curtain, which remained drawn. The house, although accoustically excellent, is so large that it requires a very strong tone and a large, simple style of playing. It is difficult, moreover, with only the violin, to appeal to an audience accustomed to voices. These considerations, as well as the uncertainty about how my playing and my compositions

ninety operas and one of the most successful of the imitators of Rossini. His son, Emilio, was the librettist for *Il Trovatore*.

[14] Spohr was curiously in error in this passage. In the original it is stated: "Two of the instruments date from the year of Stradivarius' death, in other words, from 1773, when he was an old man of ninety-three. It shows in the instruments, whose finish betrays the trembling hands of a tottering old man. The two others are from his prime, made in 1743 and 1744 and are very beautiful . . . " Stradivarius died in 1737. I have corrected the error in translating the narrative, but reproduce it here, as it was certainly an odd one for Spohr, of all people, to make.

would please the Italians, left me somewhat anxious at the outset. It was, moreover, a debut in a country where I was as yet unknown. But with the first measures I noted that the audience was receptive. My anxiety disappeared, and I played without inhibition. I also noted with pleasure that with my new concerto, written in Switzerland in the form of a *scena ed aria*, I had hit the mark. The arioso passages were received with particular enthusiasm. This noisy applause, as welcome and as encouraging as it certainly is for the soloist, is an irritant for the composer. Much of the continuity is disturbed, the carefully worked-out tuttis go unnoticed, and the audience hears the soloist re-enter in a new key without realizing that the orchestra has modulated to it.

In addition to the concerto, Dorette and I played the new Potpourri for Violin and Piano and a second Potpourri with orchestral accompaniment. This last had to be repeated. The orchestra was that of *La Scala*, and played attentively and with enthusiasm. Rolla was especially solicitous. My overture to *Alruna*[15] was played at the beginning of the second half, spiritedly if not faultlessly. The orchestra is accustomed to too many rehearsals to play flawlessly with only one. After the concert I was urged on all sides to give a second. However, since Friday is the only available day in any week, and next Friday is the Emperor's name day, with the attendant festivities, we would have to extend our stay an additional fortnight. This we do not propose to do, so a second concert will have to await our return. This first one, however, did not bring in much more than enough to cover expenses.

[15] Spohr's second opera and, like *Die Pruefung*, unperformed.

Venice, October 12, 1816

We were visited today by a German musician, Aiblinger,[16] a native of Munich and a pupil of Winter,[17] who has been living in Venice for sixteen years. He is a pianist and composer and seems to have a real feeling for his art. At least, he complained, almost with tears in his eyes, that in this country he was deprived of any opportunity of keeping pace with his German musical contemporaries. He almost never had the fortune to hear an important German work, and it simply broke his heart to be bound by his fate to a city where, for sixteen years, the same music was played over and over again, while the Germans, in the same space of time, had produced many a classic. He knows our newer music quite imperfectly from piano scores which he manages to procure from time to time at great expense of money and effort. I have subsequently had a look at his work and can testify that he might have amounted to something if he had not been cooped up in this artistic Siberia.

In order to give me some idea of the low esteen in which art and artists are held here, even by those who would like to appear as patrons, he told me what had happened to Baermann,[18] of Munich, when he was here last winter

[16] Johann Kaspar Aiblinger (1779–1867). He returned to Germany in 1819 as conductor of the Italian Opera at Munich. In 1833 he went back to Italy, settling in Bergamo and occupying himself with the collection of ancient classical music.

[17] Peter Winter (1754–1825), a prolific German composer of Italian operas. From 1798 until his death he was musical director of the Court at Munich.

[18] Heinrich Joseph Baermann (1784–1847), celebrated clarinet virtuoso. He was an intimate of Carl Maria von Weber, who described him as "a truly great artist and glorious man" and wrote some com-

with Harlass. Count Herizo, a very rich cavalier who gives two big musicales a year, with as many as two hundred listeners, invited Baermann to play at one of them. Baermann, however, had already set the date for a public concert and declined, calculating that a previous appearance would inhibit the attendance at his own concert. On the day of the latter, however, Count Herizo gave one of his own customary concerts at which Haydn's *The Creation* was performed, I believe for the first time in Venice. Baermann's concert was so ill attended that he did not even cover his expenses. Eight days later Count Herizo repeated his invitation. Baermann demanded twelve louis d'or. This was conceded, after much discussion, but Baermann learned that he was to be the victim of a joke. He withdrew in writing and left for the mainland with Harlass. After his return he was visited by a friend of Count Herizo, who wished to learn the reason for Baermann's withdrawal. When this was explained, the friend swore on his honor that he had nothing to fear, whereupon Baermann consented to play at the next concert. He was received most courteously by Count Herizo, and the music began. After about an hour, during which some six pieces had been played, Baermann became curious as to when his own turn would come. He begged a program from his neighbor and discovered to his astonishment at the end of a list of pieces that would last at least another two hours, the following words: "If time permits, Herr Baermann will play a concerto." One may imagine his anger! Count Herizo would doubtless say to him at the end of the con-

---

positions for him. Mendelssohn wrote for him the two Duets for Clarinet and Basset-horn, Opus 113.

cert: "We have no time to hear you today, maybe next time." And he would have been done out of his fee. Baermann promptly sneaked out, but had the misfortune to find the wrong exit, and landed in the canal instead of in the street. Fortunately a couple of gondoliers were on hand to fish him out. He arrived home half dead of cold and anger. Next day, Count Herizo had him summoned to the police. The Chief of Police, having heard the story, was courageous enough to take Baermann's side and to point out to Count Herizo the error of his ways. Baermann, however, thought it best to hasten his departure from Venice, particularly since some suspicious characters began making inquiries about his nightly whereabouts. Even Harlass had her troubles. She did fairly well at her debut, although taken to task for her bad accent. But at the premiere of her second opera she became so disconcerted as a result of loud talking, throat-clearing, and laughter among the listeners that she fled from the stage in the middle of her aria and collapsed behind the scenes. She developed a swollen throat and, for the remainder of the winter, could sing no more than the *secco* recitatives. All the ensembles and both finales were given without her. Yet, there being no understudy, she had to appear every evening. It should be added that the impresario, to his credit, made her no difficulties, and paid her the contracted fee.

October 15, 1816

There are two series of amateur concerts here. One series under the direction of Count Tomasini, offers a concert every two weeks at the *Teatro Fenice*. At the concert which I attended, Therese Sessi, who formerly sang in Vienna, sang two arias, a duet, and a quartet, all in her familiar style, and neither better nor worse than in Vienna. In addition to her there was an amateur who sang a number of buffo pieces in the authentic, rather exaggerated Italian manner. Everything else, particularly the overture, as regards both composition and performance, was, as usual in Italy, most wretched.

The other is a mere rehearsal series which takes place every week under the direction of Contin. The orchestra, with the exception of the basses and a few winds, consists exclusively of amateurs. It devotes itself mostly to symphonies and overtures of German masters. One can hardly speak, however, of a serious study of these works. Just getting through without breaking down is reckoned quite a success. The day I was there they played first an ancient symphony by Krommer, followed by Romberg's Symphony in E flat. At the end I was asked to conduct Beethoven's Symphony No. 2, in D, which I could not very well refuse. It was an ordeal. The orchestra was accustomed to tempi quite different from mine, and seemed unaware of the existence of distinctions between loud and soft. Everyone scraped and blew for all he was worth. The noise was such that my ears ached all night. These concerts have the virtue of acquainting the Venetian music lovers with our classical instrumental music, such as the overtures to *Don Giovanni* and *The Magic Flute*. Thus they can sense, if dimly, that the Germans, in this field, are immeasurably superior to the Italians. They admit this, to be sure, but don't really believe it, and say it only in order that they may then emphasize, without embarrassment, their own superiority in singing and in vocal composition! The smugness of the Italians, in conjunction with the paucity of their own production, is sheerly intolerable. Whenever I played one of my own compositions they knew no higher praise than to assure me that it was to the Italian taste.

October 17, 1816

Paganini returned from Trieste yesterday, apparently having given up his projected trip to Vienna. He visited me early this morning, and thus I was finally privileged to make the personal acquaintance of this prodigy about whom I have been hearing almost every day since our arrival in Italy. No instrumentalist has ever seized the imagination of the Italians as has he. Italians are not notably fond of instrumental recitals, and yet Paganini has given more than a dozen in Milan and five here. If one asks just what it is about his playing that so appeals to the Italians, one hears from the nonmusical the most exaggerated pronouncements: that he is a true magician, that he produces tones never before heard from a violin, etc. The connoisseurs, on the other hand, while granting him a certain skill in the left hand, in double-stops, and in all kinds of figuration, hold that precisely that which so charms his audiences reduces him to the level of a mere charlatan without compensating for his deficiencies in tone and interpretive style. More searching inquiry suggests that what really captures the Italian public, winning for him the sobriquet of "matchless"—which appears under his portrait—is a bag of tricks reminiscent of those with which the famous Scheller,[19] in the dark ages of good taste, used to delight the German provinces and with which he even penetrated the homes of the nobility; namely, flageolets, variations on a single string (removing the other three, in order to drive the point home), a kind of *pizzicato* with the left hand, accomplished without help of the right hand or the bow, and in many sounds not native to the violin, such as bassoon tones, the voice of an old woman, etc., etc.

As I had never heard Scheller, whose motto was "One God, one Scheller!" I was naturally curious to hear Paganini, the more so since I assumed that an artist so greatly admired could not but possess talents more substantial than those which excited so much comment. His present virtuosity is ascribed to a four-year imprisonment resulting from his having strangled his wife in a fit of passion. This, at least, was the story current both in Milan and here. Since Paganini, whose education had been neglected, could neither read nor write—so the story goes—he whiled away the hours inventing and perfecting the tricks with which he now holds all Italy by the ears.

Thanks to his unpleasant and rude behavior, Paganini had made some enemies among the local music lovers, and these, having heard me play, grasped every opportunity to praise me at his expense. This was not only unjust, since one should not draw comparison between two artists of such totally different type, but also disadvan-

[19] Jakob Scheller (1759–1803), a pupil of Viotti. In addition to the tricks mentioned by Spohr, Fétis records another in which, by loosening the strings of the bow, he was able to play on all four strings at once.

tageous for me, as it tended to make Paganini's admirers my enemies. His detractors have just published a letter in the local papers in which they say that in my style there lives again the art of the older Italian masters, Pugnani[20] and Tartini,[21] whose ample and dignified manner of playing the violin has vanished in favor of the childish exploits of contemporary virtuosos, while the Germans and the French have adapted the noble, simple style to contemporary taste. This letter, which appeared today, and of which I had no knowledge, will certainly do me more harm than good with the public here, for the Venetians are convinced that Paganini is not to be matched, much less to be surpassed.

October 19, 1816

Our concert took place yesterday, and was better attended than I had any reason to expect. Everyone was out of town who could afford a stay in the country, or who was not bound to the city by urgent business. Of all my letters of introduction I had been able to present but one, and that to the governor, Count Goes. Not that it does any good to present letters of introduction to Italians. Nothing comes of it but a chilly offer of services which they have no real desire to provide.

The theater was that of *Santa Luca*, after the *Fenice* the largest and most beautiful in Venice. The proprietor,

[20] Gaetano Pugnani (1731–1798), an important figure in the early school of Italian classical violin playing. A pupil of Somis, himself a pupil of Corelli, and later of Tartini, Pugnani was the teacher of both Polledro and Viotti.

[21] Giuseppe Tartini (1692–1770), the greatest violinist and composer for that instrument of his time.

di Vendremi, had made it available to me on the condition that I pay him two-thirds of the proceeds from the unowned boxes. It is the custom throughout Italy to sell boxes to individuals, to whom, or to whose estates, they belong as long as the theater stands. The box-owners, however, have to pay the admission price, which is low and the same throughout the house, for each performance, just as anybody else. A good deal of speculation is practiced by the box-owners, and for very popular attractions they command considerable prices. Not many boxes were taken yesterday, and di Vendremi's profits were inconsiderable.

From the coolness of the audience as I began to play, it was evident that there was some prejudice against me. This thawed, however, as the piece progressed, and at the end, the applause was so general that I was recalled time and again. What followed found the audience most receptive, and the applause was as enthusiastic as it had been in Milan. There is a very favorable notice in today's paper. It remarks, to be sure, with reference to the aforementioned letter, that it is unfair and one-sided to raise one style above the other, and that in art no one style may be accorded a monopoly. But then it goes on to say that I "combine the Italian graciousness with German seriousness" and that I "must be accorded first place among the violinists now living." In other words, praise with which any artist might well be satisfied.

October 20, 1816

Paganini came to visit me early today and had many nice things to say about the concert. I begged him to play

Karl Wilhelm Ferdinand, duke of Braunschweig, Spohr's
sponsor.

Spohr's parents.

Stadtarchiv, Braunschweig

something for me, and a number of music lovers, who happened to be with me at the moment, added their entreaties to mine. He refused flatly. Later, when we were alone, I tried again, but he told me that his style was adjusted to the requirements of a large audience, and, as such, never failed to achieve its objective; but were he to play for me he would have to play differently, and he didn't feel up to it. We would probably meet again, he said, in Rome or Naples, and then he would be more obliging. Thus, I shall probably have to leave without having heard this prodigy.

Today, as we were leaving the house, we had the wholly unexpected pleasure of encountering Meyerbeer and his whole family. He had just returned from a trip to Sicily in order to keep a rendezvous with his parents, whom he had not seen for five years, and will return by way of Florence and Rome to Naples to attend the opening of the new San Carlo Theater. It was a real pleasure to discuss matters of art with a cultivated German musician. His brother gave me the welcome news that my opera, *Faust*, had been given in Prague. He had attended a rehearsal en route. I am now impatient for news of the production.

Florence, November 5, 1816

On the day of our arrival, and almost every evening since then, we have visited the theater in the *Via della Pergola*. In production is an opera by Rossini, *L'Italiana in Algeri*, as well as a large ballet. Rossini is Italy's favorite composer, and a number of his operas, among them *Tancredi* and *Il Turco in Italia*, are given in almost every

Italian city to great applause. Having heard his compositions so highly praised in Milan and Venice, I was most
curious to hear some of them for myself. This first opera
did not entirely fulfill my expectations. It lacks, to begin
with, as is true of most Italian operas, purity of style,
characterization, and a reasonable calculation of the length
or brevity appropriate to a given scene. These characteristics, essential to any opera if it is to qualify as "classic,"
I had not, indeed, expected, since in Italy no importance
is attached to these things. One is accustomed to hearing
the same person singing now tragically, now comically,
to hear from a peasant girl the same pompous ornamentation one has just heard from a queen or a heroine, to hear
one of the principal characters sing for a quarter of an
hour at the most climactic moment, while the others
promenade in the background or talk and joke with their
colleagues in the wings. I did, however, expect attributes
which would set Rossini off from his contemporaries, particularly originality, purity of harmony, etc. But even
here I found little. What strikes the Italians as novel in
Rossini's operas is no novelty to us, mostly ideas and modulations long familiar in Germany. Nor is his harmony
by any means faultless including many shocking occur-
rences of consecutive fifths.

He is distinguished from his countrymen in respect to
rhythm and exploitation of the orchestra. His orchestra-
tion, however, compared with ours, as developed by
Mozart, still leaves a good deal to be desired. The Italians
generally stick too much to the old patterns and devices.
Violas and bassoons double the basses, while clarinets and
oboes play in unison. Since, in most Italian orchestras

there are six to eight basses to a single cello, and usually not a very good cello at that, the use of the cello for a middle voice, customary with us since Mozart's time, and so effective where appropriately introduced, is practically unknown. Nor are the winds nearly so effectively employed as in Germany. What surprised me most, in these operas, however, was the frequently awkward, uneven, melodic writing, since fluent, vocally grateful, and well-calculated melodic writing is the single praiseworthy characteristic of the new Italian opera music, and is all that compensates, more or less, for the deficiencies in other respects.

Among the singers, the prima donna, Signora Georgi, was outstanding. She has a full, strong voice with an extraordinary range of two and one-half octaves. Her part is for a deep alto, and the upper part of her range is heard, therefore, only in the ornaments. Like most singers whom I have heard in Italy, she indulges in too much ornamentation, and, therefore, gets less out of her sumptuous voice than is to be had. I am told, moreover, that she contributes nothing of her own, but rather accepts what is drilled into her, with the result that her ornaments, which are precisely the same, note for note, every night, soon become tiresome.

"The ballet, given every evening between the two acts of the opera, is the most splendid of any that I have ever seen. It is called, I believe *The Destruction of the Occidental Empire,* and is notable for its deployment of great masses in daring and surprising movements and groupings. It has been most carefully prepared, and is given every evening with the same precision. At the end comes a cavalry battle which strikes me, however, as a bit stiff and awkward."

November 8, 1816

Our concert took place last evening in the *Teatro della Pergola*. The Grand Duke,[22] to whom I had brought a letter from his brother, Rudolf, and who had several times most graciously received me, honored the occasion with his own and his entire family's presence. The small but select audience was most receptive, and was not deterred by the presence of the Grand Duke from expressing its approval in enthusiastic applause, although there was, as customary, applause for the latter, too, upon his entrance. The music sounded well in the large, sonorous theater, but the accompaniment was not of the best. Today I have received a number of proposals for a second concert next week, and shall risk it, although the Grand Duke leaves town tomorrow. Yesterday's concert, not counting a present from the Grand Duke, brought in no more than enough to cover expenses. A very favorable notice appeared in today's paper.

November 15, 1816

Our concert last night was no better attended than the first, and we made nothing on it. I am now satisfied that an instrumentalist has nothing to gain in Florence, even under the most favorable circumstances, partly because the Italians have too little respect and affection for instrumental music, partly because admission prices are set

[22] Grand Duke Ferdinand III of Tuscany, brother of Archduke Rudolf, Beethoven's pupil and patron.

too low in relation to the costs. I must note one remarkable circumstance. The violinists of the orchestra accepted no payment, an extraordinary tribute from musicians who have to live from their day-to-day earnings and who, whenever possible, charge three times too much. I should add that my playing was received with still greater applause than before. Signora Georgi sang the popular cavatina from *Tancredi*[23] very beautifully. My only complaint was that at the recapitulation of the main theme she embellished it so outrageously that the tune itself was unrecognizable.

Rome, November 22, 1816

Last evening we arrived at long last in the former capital of the world, after a long and unpleasant journey. It was unpleasant on four counts. Firstly, although we had engaged the interior of the *vetturino* for twelve louis d'or, including lodging and dinner, three additional passengers rode in the so-called cabriolet, so that we were restricted to a walking speed. Secondly, the weather was raw and, for Italy, quite cold. Our night lodgings offered little protection. Doors and windows were open, the floors were of stone, and the rooms without fireplaces. Thirdly, our quarters were consistently poor and filthy. Fourthly, the countryside through which we traveled was uninteresting and desolate. We had had a choice of two routes. The longer, by way of Perugia, is the more interesting, but requires seven days. The shorter, by way of Siena, takes six. We chose the latter. As far as Siena it was not without interest, and Siena itself is an attractive

[23] The famous aria *"Di tanti palpiti."*

town, its people having the reputation of speaking the finest Italian. From there the route was tedious, with neither houses, nor trees, nor any other sights save those sorry monuments to Roman justice, the long poles on which are hung the arms and legs of robbers and murderers. How it is possible that people should be driven to pillage and murder in a country whose soil, even without fertilizer, produces two crops a year, one of corn and one of wheat, I fail to grasp. It is so, nevertheless. As long as there is a grain surplus, the roads are safe, but as soon as there is starvation, the traveler is defenseless.

December 5, 1816

Last Sunday, Prince Friedrich of Gotha took me to the Sistine Chapel, where I saw the Pope, surrounded by the Cardinals, in full ecclesiastical magnificence, and heard the famous choir. I know not whether I am differently constituted from other tourists, or whether my expectations were too high; in any case, I found neither the music, the place, nor the ceremony either pleasing or moving. The choir consisted of some thirty persons who conducted themselves, I thought, rather boorishly. The sopranos, for the most part old men, made many mistakes, and their intonation was anything but pure. They began with some ancient two-part melodies, rather declaimed than sung. These were followed by a variety of four-part pieces with canonic entrances, which were dignified compositions in a truly churchly style and suited to the surroundings. The performances were correct, but, as I have said, rather coarse, and certainly not better than one can hear from most German choirs. The choruses alternated with three- and four-part solos. Several times we heard crescendos achieved by the gradual addition of voices, and diminuendi achieved by the same process in reverse, the device which is said to produce such a stunning effect in the Good Friday performance of the famous *Miserere!* Even now it was not ineffective, but one can hear it from any well-trained choir. The chapel is very well-suited to simple, deliberate sacred music, particularly because of the echo, which causes the voices to flow into one another. But I know several churches in Germany, notably the Palace Chapel in Wuerzburg and the Catholic church in Dresden where music sounds even better. I persuaded myself anew that vocal and instrumental music combined are more effective in the church, too, than purely vocal music, which tends to be monotonous and tiresome, its limitations being what they are. But instrumental music is forbidden in the papal chapel as incompatible with churchly etiquette.

Rome has two private musical institutions. One, a kind of choral society, has its sessions every Thursday in the home of its founder, the voice and piano teacher Sirletti. Some thirty to thirty-five singers gather there, mostly amateurs, and among them some very beautiful voices. We have now been there twice. On the first occasion they offered, in honor of the German guests, Mozart's *Requiem,* and sang it powerfully and well. The only disturbing feature was Sirletti's accompaniment from the orchestral score. I should have expected no more, for where should an Italian voice and piano teacher have obtained the requisite knowledge of harmony to read a Mozart score and play it correctly? But since I had been advised beforehand about his "profound" knowledge of harmony, I expected something better. In fact, he hit on such barbaric harmonies that Mozart, could he have heard them, would have turned over in his grave.

Last Thursday they sang two- and three-part psalms by Marcello.[24] These psalms, regarded by the Italians as classical masterpieces, and honored a few years ago by an elegant edition with long commentaries about the beauty of each, impressed me favorably, but not as favorably as all that. On the contrary, I am sure, although not intimately acquainted with German works of the same genre, that, in those of Bach and others, we possess compositions of superior quality. These psalms struck me as negligent in form. They remain too long away from the fundamental tonality and then, as soon as the tonic is regained, close immediately and most unsatisfactorily. The three-part psalms usually begin with soprano and tenor, the bass entering only at the repetition. This third voice was never essential and sounded always like the ground bass in an orchestra. And yet there were some in which the three voices were treated canonically, and these were very fine. On the whole, however, the voice-leading and modulations were monotonous, and the same entrances and retards occurred again and again. In these psalms, too, Sirletti's accompaniments were most disturbing. As with all the Italian accompanists I have heard, he has the abominable habit of doubling the bass note in the right hand, which, in certain chords, such as the six-five

[24] Benedetto Marcello (1686–1739). The reference is to Psalms from his greatest work, the *Estro poetico-armonico, parafrasi sopra i primi 50 Psalmi, poesia die Girolamo Giustiniani.* They appeared in two parts of twenty-five Psalms each in Venice, 1724–27.

chord on the leading tone, is quite unsupportable. That the resolution of such a chord leads inevitably to octaves seems not to bother these gentlemen in the least, nor to offend their ears. I was also unpleasantly impressed by the ecstatic behavior of some of the Germans present. Such grimaces! The Italians may well have imagined that we have nothing as good as this in Germany. When will the Germans ever desist from their blind admiration and imitation of everything foreign?

The second private institution meets every Monday at the home of Signor Ruffini, owner of the great catgut factory. Operas are given in concert form, again by amateurs, for an audience of from two hundred to two hundred and fifty. The singers stand on an elevated platform. The orchestra, consisting of four violins, viola, cello, bass, two clarinets, two horns, and a bassoon, surrounds them on the floor level. Last Monday, when we were introduced there by Prince Ferdinand, they did an old *opera buffa* by Paisiello.[25] This choice, for a concert performance, was less than ideal. Comic opera music can achieve its full effect only when heard in conjunction with what is seen on the stage. This particular music, even taking this disadvantage into consideration, struck me as insubstantial and dull. Singers and orchestra were equally bad. Between the acts, an amateur played the first allegro of

[25] Giovanni Paisiello (1740–1816), one of the outstanding Italian opera composers of the time, author of at least one hundred operas, and a great favorite, first of Catherine the Great, who brought him to St. Petersburg, and later of the Bonapartes, under whom he served both in Paris and Naples. He is still remembered for his lovely air, "*Nel cor piu non mi sento*," which served Beethoven for a set of variations, and which has served vocal recitalists in the conventional opening group of Italian classics ever since.

a clarinet concerto with much facility and a good tone, but without taste. He confirmed an observation that I had made previously: that the Italian virtuosos and amateurs concentrate on mechanical perfection but neglect interpretative refinement, despite the good example offered them by their best singers. Our German instrumentalists, on the other hand, develop a cultivated and expressive style on their own, without the good examples available to the Italians.

December 19, 1816

Our concert took place last evening. Since I was not permitted to give a public concert during Advent, I was obliged to arrange it privately, without public announcement. Prince Piombino arranged for us to have a room in the Ruspoli Palace, and Count Apponyi, the Austrian Minister enlisted a large number of subscriptions, so that this was the first of my concerts in Italy from which I derived a considerable income. The orchestra was drawn from the best musicians in Rome—and was the worst of any that has played for me in Italy. The ignorance, tastelessness, and impudent arrogance of these people was beyond description. Nuances of *piano* and *forte* are unknown to them. Even with this, however, one can make do. But each one makes his own embellishments according to his own dictates, with the result that the sound resembles that of an orchestra tuning up rather than a co-ordinated performance. I forbade the playing of any note not in the score, but to no avail. Free ornamentation has become so much a habit with them that they cannot do without it. One cannot imagine the noise that such an orchestra makes! As if all this were not enough, they were so unmusical and so unskilled in reading that we were time and again on the brink of disaster. Again most successful was my *Gesangsszene* and I was more highly praised for my playing of the aria than for my mastery of many more difficult things. A tenor from the Sistine Chapel, for whom I had, with the utmost difficulty obtained permission to participate, sang a duet with Fraeulein Fink, of Dresden, and a very beautiful aria by Rossini, the best piece by this composer that I have yet heard.

December 20, 1816

At the opera recently I sat next to the famous singer, Crescentini[26] (who has now completely lost his voice, although hardly fifty), and was pleased to have my judgment of the present state of music in Italy confirmed by him. His conversation reflected the unprejudiced, cultivated artist. He complained that in recent times, the good vocal school, which formerly had alone distinguished the Italians, has become ever rarer. On his last return to Italy (from Paris, I believe) he had found Italian taste so frivolous that not a trace was left of the simple, grand method of former times. For him, too, who has heard good music in Germany and France, the tedium and impression of the new Italian music is a torture.

December 27, 1816

Yesterday, at long last, the theaters were reopened, having been closed for six months. Rossini's *Tancredi* was given in the *Teatro Argentino*, the largest and most

[26] Girolamo Crescentini (1766–1846), last of the great *castrati*.

beautiful theater, while Pietro Romano's *Il Quiproquo* was given in the *Teatro Valle*. Since *Tancredi* is an old opera, and a new production of it of little interest, I was easily persuaded by Meyerbeer to accompany him to the *Teatro Valle*, while my wife and Frau Beer's children visited the *Teatro Argentino*.

Romano has taken the beloved Rossini as his model, and has imitated or copied him to such a degree that the parterre frequently broke out in cries of "Bravo, Rossini!" With all that, his writing is so faulty that an ear accustomed to pure harmony can hardly hear it without disgust. This is not necessarily a handicap in Italy, which cannot be said of the opera's want of fire and noise, which the Italians love, as, indeed, do the French and the Germans, too. Only once, after a duet, were there the reassuring shouts of "Bravo, maestro!" The composer humbly acknowledged them. All else was listened to with indifference, and at the close there was no expression, either of enthusiasm or of displeasure. The singers were very uncertain, and committed blunder after blunder. Signora Georgi, the prima donna, and the darling of last year's carnival, had no great success and was exposed, moreover, to the humiliation of seeing the seconda donna recalled after her aria in the second act, an honor not accorded her, the prima donna, the whole evenings. She gave vent to her displeasure by singing the rest of her part indifferently and in half-voice, much to the disadvantage of the ultimate finale. This contributed, doubtlessly, to the cold reception accorded the opera as a whole and to the fact that the opera is reported today to have failed. The orchestra, composed for the most part of the same "*professori*" who accompanied me, played coarsely, sloppily, and without a trace of refinement.

This morning I attended a private musicale at the home of Count Apponyi. The program consisted almost exclusively of excerpts from Rossini's operas, among which a trio—from *Elisabetta*, I think—pleased me particularly because of the good voice-leading. The more I hear of Rossini's compositions, the more I am inclined to agree, at least in part, with the general judgment that holds him to be the most distinguished of the new Italian composers and a reformer of taste in Italian opera. In all fairness, one must make an exception for Mayr,[27] who, lacking Rossini's imagination, has more knowledge and a finer esthetic feeling. Rossini, nevertheless, has discovered some new things, although not necessarily good just because they are new. Among them, for example, are what Meyerbeer so charmingly calls his "flowery melodies," which are really nothing but the old familiar figurations accompanied by syllables. Whenever such delicacies are offered by good singers, the auditorium breaks into spontaneous applause. Small wonder that Italian music becomes ever more a mere matter of ear-tickling, and singers and composers alike forget how to appeal to the heart. Thus I can say, without exaggeration, that with all the compositions I have heard thus far in Italy I have never once been moved, with the possible exception of a couple of passages in *Testa di Bronzo*.

Another Rossini novelty is the way in which he han-

[27] Simon Mayr (1763–1845), a celebrated German composer of Italian operas, of which he is credited with some seventy-eight. He is reputed to have invented the orchestral crescendo, which Rossini after him employed so effectively.

dles the parlando passages in *opera buffa*. Where formerly
a composer would employ a single tone, or, at most, adjacent intervals, Rossini exposes them to melodic excursions normally executed only in *legato*. Whether this is
good is a question. It always strikes me as bordering on
travesty, as if an instrumentalist were caricaturing a serious melody in such a way as to prompt laughter.

Also characteristic of Rossini are the *crescendo* passages that appear in almost all his works and which never
fail to carry the Italian public before them. That the *crescendos* contain many impure and offensive notes goes
without saying. Even in the first bars of the universally
admired cavatina from *Tancredi*, which was also sung
today, there occur the most horrible octaves between bass
and second oboe that I have ever heard.

In summation, my judgment of Rossini would be that
he is certainly not wanting in invention and spirit and
that if, with these attributes, he were to be thoroughly
schooled in Germany and, through Mozart's classical masterpieces, guided in the right direction, he could easily be
one of the finest vocal composers of our time. As things
now stand with him, his influence on Italian music will be
to retard it rather than to advance it. In his quest for
novelty he distances himself ever further from the simple,
great melodies of older times and never stops to think
that in so doing he is robbing the voice of its charm and
its virtue, or that he is actually degrading it when he im-
poses upon his singers roulades and passages which any
mediocre instrumentalist could manage with greater accuracy and continuity, not being required on every third
or fourth note to pronounce a syllable. With his "flowery

song," regardless of the pleasure it excites, he is well on the way to putting an end to real song, of which not much is left in Italy anyway. The contemptible crowd of his imitators are helping him.

December 29, 1816

Meyerbeer and I went last night to hear *Tancredi* at the *Teatro Argentino*. A more miserable performance I have never heard. God have mercy on the composer whose work falls into such hands! It would be unjust to speak of a work on the basis of such a distortion, particularly since many numbers were omitted and others added. . . .

December 30, 1816

I am convinced that the Italians are not lacking in the qualities essential for the study of the fine arts. Indeed, they may even surpass their northern neighbors in native capacity. Most of their singers have a good ear for intonation and the ability to sing a melody accurately after a single hearing, although the majority are uneducated to the extent of being unable to read music. At Count Apponyi's last musicale, they tried a canon by Cherubini. Moncade, the celebrated tenor, was asked to participate, of whom I had heard that he was among those who could not read. When he promptly volunteered to sing something he could not have known, I assumed the charge to be false. And, indeed, he began well. The Countess played the slow, eight-measure melody through, and Moncade repeated it note for note, including all the little ornaments with which she had adorned it. But when he entered upon the second voice, he could get no further with the notes and sang by ear, achieving something that had little resemblance to Cherubini. When the third singer, also a non-reader entered and, after singing the simple melody, went his own way, the confusion and discord were such that an end had to be put to it. Neither singer was particularly embarrassed. They said they had hoped that it "might go." They reminded me of the Englishman who, when asked if he could play the violin, said: "Quite possibly, I've never tried."

Naples, February 1, 1817

Naples is undistinguished by beautiful architecture, but because of its situation and many individual characteristics, must be counted among the most beautiful cities of the world. Coming from Rome one misses the full flavor of antiquity in the buildings and other objects which will make that city forever the goal of the student of architecture, sculpture, and painting. But in Naples one is compensated by other virtues. The amphitheatrical setting assures am imposing view, while the flat roofs and the cupolas and towers, covered with lackered, vari-colored brick, give the city an unusual, oriental appearance. It is, moreover, one of the world's liveliest cities, certainly one of the noisiest. Although Vienna and Hamburg, the largest cities of my experience, probably number about as many inhabitants as Naples, the latter seems incomparably livelier, due probably in part to the southern temperament of its citizens, in part to the fact that all classes prefer to roam the streets rather than stay at home and work. The noise in these streets is beyond description. Until one has become accustomed to it, the effect is sheerly deafening.

Spohr as General Music Director. From an oil painting by
Emilie von der Embde.

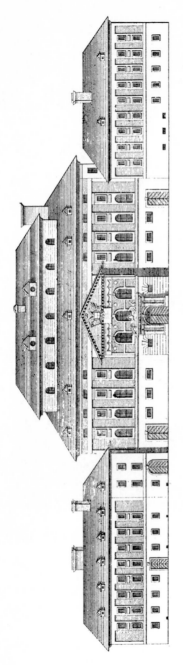

Theater an der Wien as it appeared in Spohr's time. It still stands.

All the craftsmen have their shops on the street, black-smiths, locksmiths, coppersmiths, cabinetmakers, tailors, and cobblers. Everyone sits in front of his house in one grand community and works. Add to that the rattling of the wagons and fiacres, almost always two abreast, the cries of the tradesmen hawking their wares, each trying to outshout the other, and finally the animated talk of those who meet one another in the street! As to the latter, what the uninitiated German takes to be a quarrel turns out to be nothing more than an innocent discussion of the weather and the latest gossip of the day. More striking than in any other city in the world is the contrast between rich and poor, among the latter specially the so-called *lazzaroni,* of whom one sees whole families lying in the streets, surrounded by high society, picking lice from their half-naked bodies. A more repulsive sight I have never seen!

February 15, 1817

Now that I have been a few times to the *San Carlo,* I feel that I am in a position to pass judgment on it. On my first visit it was as with St. Peter's. It seemed nothing like as large as it really is. I had to be assured again and again that it is four feet wider and I don't know how many feet longer than *La Scala* at Milan before I could believe it. But when the curtain was raised and I could measure individual persons against the objects represented in the scenery, I realized that here, too, I had been deceived by the good proportions of the colossal details. Here, for the first time, people, standing in the remotest reaches of the stage, appeared in a reasonable relationship to their sur-soundings. I know no better place for ballet and panto-mime. Military movements of infantry and cavalry, bat-tles, and storms at sea can be represented here without falling into the ludicrous. But for opera, itself, the house is too large. Although the singers, Signora Colbran[28] and the Signori Nozzari, Benedetti, etc., have very strong voices, only their highest and most stentorian tones could be heard. Any kind of tender utterance was lost. Before the fire, it is said, the theater was as sonorous as *La Scala*. The unfortunate deterioration is attributed to three fac-tors: (1) the proscenium has been widened by a few feet, (2) the roof is not as arched as formerly, and (3) the pro-truding stucco ornaments inhibit the tone and throw it back. If the house was really so sonorous before the fire, the improvements sought in the new construction have not materialized. Rather the reverse. The authorities would be well advised to throw out the superfluous deco-ration, which is heavy and not in the best of taste, and try to regain some of the building's former virtues.

The first opera I saw was *Gabriele di Vergi*, by Count Caraffa,[29] formerly an amateur, now, as an impecunious younger son of the family, a professional artist, depend-ent upon his craft for his daily bread. The opera pleased me, without moving me particularly. The style is heavy,

[28] Isabella Angela Colbran (1785–1845), a pupil of Crescentini and one of the most celebrated singers of her time. She and Rossini were married in 1822.

[29] Michele Enrico Caraffa di Colobrano (1787–1872), a Napoleonic officer who turned to composition as a profession after Napoleon's fall. He later became a pupil and protégé of Cherubini in Paris and pro-duced a number of successful but short-lived operas.

with a tendency to overpower the singers. The performance was quite precise on the part both of the singers and of the orchestra. The latter, under the exact, fiery direction of Signor Festa,[30] was well prepared, although wanting in nuances of *piano* and *forte;* the wind instruments, particularly were too strong. Of the singers there is little more to say than that they have good, strong voices. Whether or not they have good interpretive style is, in this theater, impossible to say, since one either hears them shout or doesn't hear them at all. After the opera they gave the ballet *Cinderella,* staged by Duport, with a great investment of scenery, costumes, and supers. Aside from Duport and his wife, the dancer, Vestris, was outstanding.

Another opera, also by an amateur, Carlo Saccenti, was given a week ago, after three months of study and rehearsal. The King, whose protege the composer is, had selected it for the opening of the new *San Carlo.* Mayr, who had been summoned to Naples by the impressario to write a new opera for the opening, had to stand aside with his own. Later, when it became apparent that Saccenti's opera could not possibly be made ready for the opening, Mayr was pressed into service to compose a cantata, with which the theater was, indeed, opened on January 12. According to the connoisseurs, this cantata, although hurriedly written, contained much beautiful music. However, since the text, devoted to the burning of the theater, was ill suited to a musical setting, the effect was not extraordinary. Nor was Mayr helped by the fact that the

[30] Giuseppe Maria Festa (1771–1839), musical director at the Court of Naples and a reputable violin virtuoso.

public's attention was diverted by the brilliant lighting and the formal ceremony accompanying the attendance of the court.

With the opening behind them, the theater directors turned again to Saccenti's opera. What leaked out to the public from these rehearsals was highly contradictory. The composer's friends insisted that he had accomplished something which, by its originality and excellence, would bring about a reform of the entire Italian lyric theater. The singers and musicians, on the other hand, let it be known that they had never in all their lives sung or played anything so boring and inept as this miserable opera. The unbiased assumed that the truth, as usual, would lie between the extremes. The few rehearsals which I attended left me wholly on the side of the singers and the instrumentalists. One would be hard put to it to write anything worse, even if the objective were to contradict every rule which experience has taught us with respect to rhythm, melodic structure, harmony, and instrumentation. There was not a trace of melody, nor of the prosecution of an idea, but every three measures something new, and with the faultiest modulations. Right in the introduction there are three ugly fifths in a row. According to one of the musicians, the composer defended this phenomenon most ingeniously by reference to the English sailor who, accused of having three wives, was acquitted on the grounds that the law expressly forbade any man to have "two wives at one time," but said nothing of three. Similarly, said the composer, it is forbidden to write two fifths, one after the other, but nothing is said of three.

The performance finally took place, after countless rehearsals, in the presence of the court and a crowded house. Despite the stiff Spanish etiquette which prescribes the form here—for example, it is required that the curtain be raised upon the King's arrival in his box, placing the poor singers in the unhappy situation of having to stand and be looked at during the playing of the overture, and every expression of displeasure or approval is forbidden—despite these restrictions, which inhibit an unbiased judgment, the opera was hooted down. A similar fate befell it the next night, not a single one of the composer's friends daring to applaud. With this second performance, which I attended, the opera was buried. The composer attributes its failure to the ignorance of the Neapolitan public and will bring it to Germany. The blessings of Apollo and the Muses be upon it!

February 20, 1817

The carnival ended day before yesterday and the fast has begun. After the din of the last days of the carnival, the quiet, which has now set in, is doubly welcome, although the evenings are a little dull, the theaters being closed for four days. At the *San Carlo*, this year, opera is being given in place of the usual oratorios, although without ballets, which are utterly forbidden in this season. At the *Teatro Fiorentino* they gave an opera, *Paolo e Virgina*, by the younger Guglielmi,[31] not without some success. It has quite a few pleasant numbers, none of them particularly notable. The third act is distinguished by

---

[31] Pietro Carlo Guglielmi (1763–1827), son of the more famous Pietro Guglielmi (1727–1804), who had been an important rival of Paisiello and Cimarosa in Naples in the preceding generation.

some characteristically Italian tastelessness where Paul, during a storm at sea, sings an aria in the customary form, with the equally customary instrumental interludes and the equally customary vocal trills and figurations, when he would better be employed coming to the assistance of his beloved. This storm at sea, without any trace of appropriate music, was the most ludicrous thing I have ever experienced in the theater. In this theater, with a full house, we found for the first time in Italy, a quiet and attentive public.

The end of the carnival was far less riotous than I had anticipated. About all it amounted to was that half of Naples, masked and unmasked, in carriages and on foot, crowded into the *Via Toledo*, moving back and forth, bombarding one another with little plaster balls. Even the masked balls at the *San Carlo* are said to have been rather dull. There was no want of inventive costumes, but, apparently, a total want of the wit and talent required to continue from costume to a full characterization.

February 26, 1817

I have been twice to the Conservatory. The first time was for a student's concert where a number of overtures or first movements of symphonies by one of the students, the first violinist, in fact, were rehearsed. These pieces were not without invention, although patterned in form and instrumentation on the overtures of Rossini, which I would hardly suggest as fitting models. The playing was very mediocre. There young people have no schooling, least of all the violinists and cellists. The former do not know how to hold either violin or bow and, therefore, play neither distinctly nor clearly. With the instruction which they receive it could hardly be otherwise. Festa, the only well-schooled violinist here, is not employed at the Conservatory. It is also most blameworthy that the young people do not give their students' concerts under the supervision of their teachers; their first violinist and director, who is also a student, has neither the repose nor the experience for such a task. At the second concert which I attended, a couple of singers appeared. They had neither good voices nor good schooling. Everything I have heard here is far beneath the standard of the Milan students. Signor Zingarelli,[32] director of the Conservatory and professor of theory and singing, may have made his contributions as an opera composer, but it is generally conceded that the Conservatory has fallen off since his assumption of the directorship. That he does not know how an orchestra should be conducted, or a symphony played, is evident from the fact that he complacently permits the scandal to continue. Of the accomplishments of our German composers he has very odd notions. When I visited him he spoke highly of Haydn and certain other composers without ever mentioning the name of Mozart. When I mentioned it, he commented that Mozart had "not been without talent, but had lived too short a time to cultivate it properly; had he been able to study for another ten years, he would probably have written something decent." An ass!

[32] Nicola Antonio Zingarelli (1752–1837), a celebrated composer of operas and sacred music, and, like Paisiello, a favorite of Napoleon. Before returning to his native Naples, he succeeded the elder Guglielmi as musical director of the Sistine Chapel. From 1813 on, he was not only director of the Conservatory, but also musical director of the Court Orchestra.

March 3, 1817

An opera by Mayr, *Cora,* written some years ago, has been restaged. It has a number of agreeable episodes, but does not, on the whole, fulfill the expectations I had entertained of Mayr's music. He has become inextricably identified with the Italian style, and there is now next to nothing in his music to betray his German origin. His melodic line and his instrumentation are wholly Italian. This is hardly surprising when one remembers that he has been living in Italy since his fourteenth year and has never written for any but Italian audiences. My guess is that, quite aside from his native talent, he has distinguished himself from his colleagues by the assiduous study (sometimes, doubtless, too assiduous) of the works of the German masters. He is beloved throughout Italy, and here particularly, and not without reason. As a person he is still the thorough, conscientious, simple, modest German. He still loves his fatherland, and seems to regret only that it was not his fate to make his career as a composer in Germany. He intends now to settle down in retirement in Bergamo, where he is musical director, and to compose only for his church. He assured me that only the honor of writing for the opening of the *San Carlo* had tempted him to leave his asylum in Bergamo once more, and that this opera, *The Revenge of Juno,* which he had just finished, would certainly be his last. In *Cora* the most popular piece with the public is the finale, consisting of a theme and variations in the old Pleyel style; one singer presents the theme, the second does a variation in eighth notes, the third, in triplets, and the last in sixteenths. Well sung, it has a great effect—and criticism had better be silent.

March 6, 1817

Last evening Pio Chianchettino gave a concert in the *Teatro Fondo*. He is a nephew and pupil of Dussek, and played two of the latter's concertos, very much in his style. Although his playing was clear, articulate, and even expressive, it confirmed my experience both here and elsewhere that the piano, as solo instrument in concertos, leaves the listeners cold, the more so the larger the hall. In this concert, as on other occasions, the vocal pieces were much better liked than the concertos, although no one took exception to his playing. This applied to me, too. As much as I love the piano when an inventive pianist improvises, it leaves me cold as a concert instrument. In my opinion a piano concerto can be effective when written in the manner of the Mozart concertos with the piano hardly more prominent than any other instrument in the orchestra. . . .

March 11, 1817

We gave our concert last night in the ballroom of the *San Carlo*. With an attentive audience, admirably supported by the orchestra under Festa, and favored by the size and character of the room, I played better than in any of the other cities of Italy. Aside from my own pieces, there was a duet by Mayr and a trio by Cherubini, sung by Davide, Nozzari, and Benedetti. Afterward I was overwhelmed with demands to give a second concert.

March 22, 1817

Since I was disinclined to go the trouble of arranging a second concert, I accepted the suggestion of the impre-

183

sario of the *San Carlo* to appear as soloist between the acts. The first of these appearances took place yesterday. I was much concerned about the capacity of the violin to fill so large a house, and was relieved when, after the rehearsal, I was assured that the tone was distinctly heard in the remotest corners of the house. I had to forego the more delicate nuances, of course. Although the house was full, there was complete silence during my playing, and I was recalled after the second piece. . . . I have played my quartets and quintets a number of times in private houses, most recently at the home of the Marquise Douglas. She plays piano well and is said to have once sung most excellently. She and her husband are the first English people in whom I have found a true feeling for music.

March 23, 1817

In leafing through this diary I note that I have forgotten to mention the performances of two masses under the auspices of Prince Esterhazy. The first, an old favorite in Vienna, was undistinguished. The second, however, Haydn's Mass in D minor,[33] given with much solemnity and military pomp on the Emperor's birthday, was a true artistic delight. Chorus, orchestra, and soloists all distinguished themselves. Unfortunately, at the express order of the Prince, the tempi were uniformly too fast, which spoiled a good deal of it.

Milan, April 22, 1817

Because of the press of business during the last days of our sojourn in Naples, and our hurried, almost nonstop

[33] It was the *Nelson* Mass.

return to Milan, I have fallen behind in my writing and now have a good deal to catch up with, including much that still happened in Naples.

Mayr's new opera was finally given a fortnight before Easter and was such a dismal failure that it was taken off after three and one-half performances and buried, probably forever. At the third performance only one act was given, the program being filled out by an act from Paer's *Sargino*. Both the subject matter and the music of Mayr's opera were equally dull. The music had neither life nor fire. It was so ordinary and so drawn-out that it was difficult to hear without falling asleep. Mayr seems to have exhausted himself, which is hardly surprising in view of the incredible number of operas he has written. It is high time that he retired as an opera composer before he compromises his well-earned fame, and he would probably have been well advised to decline this last summons to Naples. He departed for Bergamo immediately after the premiere.

The arrival of Signora Catalani[34] had all the music lov-

[34] Angelica Catalani (1780–1849), a very celebrated soprano. Spohr adds to her age, which was only thirty-six at the time, but it should be remembered that singers began earlier in those days and that Catalani herself made her debut at the age of sixteen. Lord Edgcumbe, who heard her eleven years later at Plymouth, is quoted by Grove as observing: "Her voice is of a most uncommon quality, and capable of exertions almost supernatural . . . while its agility in divisions, running up and down the scale in semi-tones, and its compass in jumping over two octaves at once, are equally astonishing. It were to be wished that she was less lavish in the display of these wonderful powers, and sought to please more than to surprise; but her taste is vicious, her excessive love of ornament spoiling every simple air, and her greatest delight (indeed, her chief merit) being songs of a bold and spirited character, where much is left to her discretion (or indiscretion), without being confined by the accompaniment, but in which she can indulge in ad

ers of Naples in a great state of excitement. She took advantage of it, and promptly arranged a concert in the *Teatro Fiorentino* with tickets at seven times the normal price. The day before the concert it was only with the greatest difficulty that I was able to get two tickets, and then only because I had ordered them in advance. Never has an audience been in such a state of intense expectation as the Neopolitan audience that evening. Even my wife and I, who had hoped for years to have the opportunity of hearing this admired singer, could hardly contain ourselves. At long last she appeared, and there was a deathly stillness throughout the auditorium. Her bearing was cold and rather pretentious, and she greeted neither the Court nor the rest of the audience, which made an unpleasant impression. Possibly she had expected in her own turn, to be greeted with applause, which is not customary in Naples, and was piqued when there was none. Her first song, however, was fervently applauded, and she promptly became more friendly, remaining so the rest of the evening. She sang four times—two arias by Pucitta,[35] the "*Ombra adorata*"[36] of Zingarelli (or, according to the Neopolitans, of Crescentini, whose name was on the program), and Variations on the long-suffering "*Nel cor piu non mi sento.*" The Pucitta arias were miserable; the famous "*Ombra adorata*" can be enjoyed only if one forgets the text; the variations were commonplace, although given a

---

libitum passages with a luxuriance and redundancy no other singer ever possessed, or if possessing ever practised, and which she carries to a fantastical excess."

[35] Vincenzo Pucitta (1778–1861), Italian opera composer, who also traveled with Catalani as her accompanist.

[36] An aria from Zingarelli's *Romeo and Juliet.*

certain piquancy by the manner of their delivery. There was much sheer pleasure in the purity of her intonation, in the perfection of every kind of figuration and embellishment, and the individuality of her interpretive style. But she was not quite the prototype of the perfect singer upon which we had counted. Her voice has a respectable range from G below the staff to the B above, and in the lower and middle registers, the voice is full and strong. The passage to the upper register around E and F, however, is quite conspicuous, and three or four tones in this area are noticeably weaker than the very low and the very high. In order to cover up this defect she sings all the figures that occur here in half-voice. Nor does her voice have a youthful sheen, which is scarcely to be wondered at in a singer forty years old. Her trill is especially beautiful, whether in whole or semi-tones. Much admired was a run through the half-tones, actually an enharmonic scale, since each half-tone occurred twice. This is regarded as something exclusively hers. I found it more remarkable than beautiful, sounding something like the howling of the wind in a smokestack. Very beautiful was the way in which she accomplished another, and not uncommon type of ornamentation, a descending scale of coupled eighths and sixteenths, pausing for breath after each sixteenth and giving to the whole passage a most melancholy complexion. Among the variations was one in syncopation, which had a strikingly individual character, and another in triplets, which she managed with the utmost perfection. What I missed most in her singing was soul. Her recitatives were rendered without expression, almost carelessly, and her adagios left one cold. We were never once moved, but we did have the pleasure always associated with the spectacle of the easy mastery of mechanical difficulties. I must still mention certain unpleasant and obtrusive mannerisms which, at her age, she can hardly be expected to overcome. Among them is the habit, in passages, and particularly in full voice, of chewing out each tone in such a way that even a stone-deaf listener, if he saw her sing, could distinguish between eighths and sixteenths as she goes up and down the scale. Particularly in trills the movement of her chin is such that each note can be counted. Secondly, in passionate episodes, she indulges in bodily movements, possibly Latin, but certainly unwomanly, from which, again, a deaf person could easily divine the figures she is singing.

A few days later we heard her again at the rehearsal for her second concert. She sang five times, demonstrating the same virtues and the same incapacity to move deeply. She seemed, on this occasion, much less pretentious, much more engaging. She was also most gracious to the orchestra and to the people who had crowded in to hear her. Thus I was quite ready to believe what various persons told me; namely, that her pretentious bearing at her first appearance had proceeded rather from embarrassment than from pride, and was essentially a device for disguising her anxiety. A young man who had been backstage at that first concert assured me that at her first entrance she had trembled from head to foot, and had hardly been able to breathe, so intense was her nervousness.

Here in Milan, I am told, she had no great success, and her later concerts were less well-attended than the first. A faction among the public sided with Grassini,[37] whose partisans played Catalani a mean trick by translating her unfavorable notices from Hamburg and Leipzig into Italian and distributing them at the entrance before her concert. Even Catalani, expecting a sonnet or something of the kind in her honor, bought a copy.

The day following Catalani's concert, Rossini's *Elisabetta* was given at the *San Carlo* with Colbran in the title role. Since everyone knew that she was out to compete with Catalani, the house was unusually full, with not only Colbran's partisans but also her enemies represented. The latter had not hesitated to describe the previous evening as "Colbran's requiem," and everyone was curious to see what Colbran would do about it. At her first entrance she was greeted by a mixture of hoots and applauses. As the evening wore on, however, with Colbran singing and acting most beautifully, the hoots diminished and the applause increased, until, at the end, she was unanimously recalled. She is rather inferior to Catalani in voice and lacks her mechanical perfection, but sings with true feeling and acts with passion. The opera, among Rossini's best, has the usual defects as well as the usual virtues. During the intermission they were telling of a ludicrous example of Catalani's self-importance: a few evenings before, when she visited the theater for the first time, she sent her secretary backstage between the acts to tell Colbran and the rest of the cast that Catalani "was well pleased with their performance!"

[37] Josephina Grassini (1773–1850), considered at one time the first singer in Italy. She was also a great favorite in London and Paris, where she commanded fees as high as Catalani's.

Aachen, August 10, 1817

Here at last I have a few moments' time in which to continue the story of our return journey from Italy.

On April 3 we finally heard the *Miserere*[38] at the Sistine Chapel. We had been told that ladies should have tickets of admission and that men had to have shoes. Unfortunately, not a ticket was to be had, and I had no choice but to go alone. At the entrance to the church, however, I noticed an acquaintance among the Swiss guards, a man whose favor I had earned by rewarding him with a present for having guided me through the dome of St. Peter's. I asked him if he could not help me get my wife in without a ticket. He assured me that he would do his best, and I hurried off to fetch her. After a good deal of palaver with the other Swiss guards we managed to get in, although a number of English ladies of high position, who had come without tickets, were denied admission. It seems that the Swiss cannot abide the French and the English, and favor the Germans, particularly if one can speak a few words of Swiss German. We arrived in good time and regretted only that we could not remain together and exchange opinions immediately on all that transpired.

Before the beginning of the music nineteen psalms were rendered, alternately by high and low voices in unison, and in the same manner that we had found so tiresome Christmas. There were still eight or nine to go when we

[38] From the musical examples cited by Spohr in an article he wrote on this experience for the *Allgemeine Musikalische Zeitung*, the editor of the *Baerenreiter* Edition concludes that what he heard was a five-voiced Mass by Giuseppe Baini (1775–1844), one time master of the papal choir, described by Grove as "a cinque-cento priest of the higher order born out of time."

arrived. The psalms lasted about five minutes each, and at the close of each a candle was extinguished on the great candelabra before the High Altar. How one prayed for the last of them to go! Finally the great moment arrived, and an expectant stillness gripped the assemblage. This tension of the solemn twilight in the church, now lighted only by the last rays of the setting sun, and the quiet, coming after the rumbling psalms, doubtless explains the benevolent effect which the first, sustained C minor chord had upon me. It seemed like music from another world. One was quickly reminded, however, that it was, indeed, an earthly music, and sung by Italians; for in the second measure the ear was assaulted by the most atrocious fifths! I would hardly have trusted the evidence of my own ears that such a thing was possible in the Sistine Chapel, had I not heard the same passage repeated. Is this then the secret manner of presenting this old music, which it is said that only this choir knows, and then only because it has been passed down from generation to generation? It cannot be so! Only modern Italians could sing so barbarically. They have a feeling for melody, but are unbelievably ignorant about harmony.

Once I had recovered from this first painful shock, I began again to be drawn to the music. The simple progressions, mostly triads; the interweaving of the voices, now rising to a thundering *forte*, now vanishing in the softest *pianissimo;* the endless sustaining of single tones, which only a castrato's lungs could support; and, finally, the delicate attack on a new chord while the previous one is still fading away—all this gives to this music, despite the deficiencies of performance, something so unique and individual that one is irresistibly drawn to it. I can well believe that in former times, when the choir was better, it must have made a tremendous impression upon visitors, particularly upon those who had never heard *a cappella* music and the voices of castrati. It could have such an effect even now if the singers had a knowledgeable director. As it is, they do not even sing in tune.

[The remainder of this entry, the last of the diary of the Italian tour, recounts the details of the Spohr's return to Germany. The route was roughly the same as that of the journey south, and is without musical interest. In Geneva they ran out of money, but were able to save their situation by borrowing from a friend. From Geneva they continued northward, stopping in Thierachern to pick up their belongings, including Dorette's harp. They gave concerts in Freiburg, Karlsruhe, Wiesbaden, and Ems without much financial success. Not until Aachen were they able to attract an audience of sufficient size to make possible the repayment of the Geneva debt. They remained in Aachen until autumn.—H. P.]

INTERVAL

THE SPOHRS MADE A SHORT AND PROFITABLE TOUR of Holland in the fall of 1817, during which Spohr was offered and accepted the directorship of the Theater in Frankfurt am Main. He remained in Frankfurt until the fall of 1819, when differences between him and the directors led to his resignation. There followed the journey to London, recounted in the following pages.

VIII

JOURNEY TO LONDON

(1819–20)

Prior to my departure from Frankfurt, I had accepted an engagement with the Philharmonic Society of London[1] for the following Parliament season, extended to me by Ferdinand Ries,[2] the famous piano virtuoso and composer, on behalf of the society. The latter had been founded a few years before by a group of the most famous artists of London, among them Clementi, the two Cramers,[3] Moscheles,[4] Ries, Potter, and Smart,[5] for the purpose of

[1] Founded in 1813.

[2] Ferdinand Ries (1784–1838), a pupil of Winter in composition and of Beethoven on piano, one of the most celebrated pianists and composers of his time. He was a dominant figure in London musical life in the decade between 1814 and 1824.

[3] Franz Cramer (1772–1848) and Johann Baptist Cramer (1771–1858), distinguished German musicians who spent the greater part of their careers in London. J. B. Cramer, a pupil of Clementi, is considered, along with his teacher, to have been one of the principal founders of modern piano playing. His studies are used in piano teaching to this day. The younger brother, Franz, was a violinist.

[4] Ignaz Moscheles (1794–1870), one of the most reputable German

giving a series of eight concerts during the session of Parliament. The demand for subscriptions, despite the high cost of tickets, was so great that several hundred subscribers could not be accommodated and had to take their places on a waiting list. The Society's resources were, accordingly, such that it could engage, not only the best singers and instrumentalists of London as soloists, but also distinguished artists from abroad.

Thus it was that I was engaged for the season of 1820. Against a substantial fee, covering travel over and back and a four-months' subsistence in London, I had a fourfold obligation: to conduct some of the concerts, to appear as soloist in several, to play in the violin section in all of them, and, finally, to offer one of my orchestra compositions to the society as its permanent property. In addition to my fee, I was guaranteed a benefit concert in the hall of the society, with its orchestra participating. Although my wife was not included in these arrangements I could not bring myself to leave her for four months. Our family council therefore decided that she would accompany me and that she would appear as harpist in London, at least in my own concert. As the season began in February and the crossing of the channel would fall in the rawest season of the year, we decided further to go by way of Calais and, in order to concertize in the Belgian and French towns along the way, to set forth six to eight weeks ahead of time.

piano virtuosos and teachers of his time, of which a considerable part was passed in England. He was one of Mendelssohn's piano teachers.

[5] Sir George Smart (1776-1867), English conductor and composer, one of the founders of the Philharmonic Society, and for many years one of its principal conductors.

We went first to Gandersheim to my parents, who were to take the children during our absence. From there we went to Hamburg where we gave two concerts with great success. I also played my new quartets, which had been published there, for sophisticated audiences, most excellently accompanied. Both quartets were also played on several occasions. I found the enthusiasm for this form greater in Hamburg than anywhere else with the possible exception of Vienna.

We continued our tour to Berlin, Dresden, Leipzig, Kassel, etc., giving concerts in each city. Of these concerts I have neither memory nor record except for the following notice from Berlin, dated November 4, 1819:

"The writer, after an interval of ten years, still treasures a most vivid recollection of the masterly, thoughtful compositions of Herr Spohr—replete with harmonic profundity and imaginative modulation—not to mention his violin playing, unique of its kind. Nevertheless, it seems to him now that the fullness and sweetness of tone which this sensitive artist draws from his violin, and his exemplary projection of the cantabile are an improvement even over his former achievements. His admirable finish in octaves and tenths, in double-, triple-, and even quadruple-stops, his ease and security in the most daring leaps, his free bowing, and his unmannered, dignified deportment—all these virtues so seldom united in a single executive and creative artist, reflect German industry, genius, and high purpose in a nature predisposed for a superior dedication to the much abused art of music. . . . Madame Spohr's delicate playing was sovereign over all the difficulties of modulation, even in the remotest tonalities, and demonstrated a most satisfactory communion of virtuosity and good taste. Her husband's compositions were most attractive. The manner in which this modest couple were now united in tender harmony, then engaged in the stormy flight of bold fantasy, was most pleasantly effective."

In Brussels we encountered another touring couple who, like ourselves, played violin and harp. They were Alexander Boucher[6] and his wife, from Paris. I had already heard a good deal about them, and was therefore curious to make their personal acquaintance. Boucher was reputed to be both an excellent violinist and something of a charlatan. He bore a striking resemblance to Napoleon in both face and figure, and exploited it to the utmost. He had practiced to perfection the postures of the exiled Emperor, his manner of wearing a hat, and his way of taking snuff. When he arrived in a new city he would perform these imitations on the promenade or in the theater in order to draw attention to himself. He even spread the rumor that this resemblance was disturbing to the present authorities, because of the people's affection for Napoleon, and that he was about to be banished. In Lille, at least, as I later learned, he had announced his last concert in the following manner: *"Une malheureuse ressemblance me force de m'expatrier; je donnerai donc, avant de quitter ma belle patrie, un concert d'adieux, . . ."* The placards for this concert contained another example of charlatanism: *"Je jouerai ce fameux concerto de Viotti, en mi-*

[6] Alexandre Jean Boucher (1778-1861). In addition to the eccentricities described by Spohr, he used to climax a furious passage by upsetting the bridge of his violin. His wife complemented him in such excursions by playing duets for harp and piano with one hand on each instrument.

mineur, dont l'exécution à Paris m'a gagné surnom: l'Alexandre des violons."

I was on the point of looking up Boucher when he beat me to it. He most kindly offered to be of assistance in the arrangements for my concert and, aside from his boasting, was most pleasant. He introduced us to several music-loving families who, in turn, afforded us the opportunity to hear the Bouchers at their musicales.

Their playing together was distinguished by much virtuosity, but what they played was trivial, whether by Boucher or not I no longer remember. Before they joined forces, Boucher played a quartet by Haydn, adding so many inappropriate and tasteless embellishments that it was impossible for me to have any pleasure from it. Most striking was the way in which Boucher allowed himself to be waited upon by his wife. When he had taken his place at the music stand for the quartet, she asked him for the key to his violin case. She opened it, took out the violin, then the bow, which she rubbed with resin, laid the notes on the stand and then took a seat beside him in order to turn pages. When we were asked to play, the reverse procedure took place. Not only did I take my own instrument from its case but also my wife's, carrying it to the spot where we would play, and tuning it. Madame Boucher had done all this herself. I should add here that I always tuned my wife's harp at our public concerts, not only to spare her the trouble, but also in order to be sure of an exact tempered tuning, which, as is generally known, is not so easy. We played one of our brilliant duets and earned much applause. Boucher seemed delighted with my playing, and well may have meant it, for in a letter of introduction to the Baron d'Assignies in Lille, which the latter subsequently showed me as a curiosity, he said, after describing my playing: "... *enfin, si je suis, comme on le prétend, le Napoléon des violons, M. Spohr est bien le Moreau!*"

My concert took place in the new large theater to great applause. The income, however, after deduction of the very considerable expenses, was small, as our fame had not preceded us to Brussels. We were urged by the public and the critics to give a second concert, but couldn't find a suitable date. As our lodgings in the large hotel where we had stopped were expensive, we chose to continue to Lille without further delay.

My first visit upon our arrival there was to Herr Vogel, who had been described to me as the best violinist in town and conductor of the local Amateur Concerts. He was not at home, but I was received most graciously by Madame Vogel. When I mentioned my name her face became transfigured and she asked excitedly if I were the composer of the Nonet, the theme of which she sang. When I responded in the affirmative she fell on my neck in a burst of Gallic impulsiveness and cried: "Oh! how pleased my husband will be, *car il est fou de votre Nonetto!*" No sooner had I returned to the inn that Vogel appeared, his face radiant with pleasure, and bid me welcome as if I had been an old friend.

We experienced many happy hours in the home of this worthy couple. Vogel promptly arranged a concert for us in the hall of the Amateur Society, as all its members were most eager to see and hear the composer of the much played Nonet. Our success, particularly in those things we did together, was such that a date was immediately set for a second concert. Some music lovers from neighboring Douay, who had come over for the concert, invited us to play there, with a guaranteed sale of four hundred tickets. Thus, I had excellent prospects of realizing a good deal of money in Lille when an unexpected event intervened. The carriage was loaded and we were set to leave for Douay when a rumor spread through town that the Duc de Berry had been murdered.[7] The rumor was soon officially confirmed. As this put an end to any further concertizing in France and as it was not yet time to continue on to England, we were easily persuaded to stay on in Lille.

There was music-making almost every day in private houses, and I found occasion to introduce all my quartets, quintets, and harp compositions to this circle of enthusiastic music lovers. They were a most receptive and grateful audience, and I still remember these musicales with much pleasure.

I also heard many stories of Boucher. It was told of him that once when a certain passage had not come off to his satisfaction, he stopped, without reference to the accompanying orchestra, and cried, *"Cela n'a pas réussi, allons, Boucher, encore une fois!"* And there was the incident at the end of his second and last concert. The final number was a rondo of his own composition, which included an improvised cadenza just before the end. At the rehearsal he had demonstrated to the orchestra the trill

[7] The Duc de Berry was assassinated Februry 13, 1820, in the Paris Opera House.

which would signal the end of the improvization and had arranged to cue in their attack for the final tutti by stamping his foot. On the night of the concert it was already quite late when the time for this concluding rondo arrived, and the good amateurs already had their minds on their suppers rather than their work. Boucher's cadenza, in which, once again, he paraded all his tricks, seemed endless, and some of the gentlemen simply put their instruments in their cases and sneaked away. The example was infectious, and in a few minutes the entire orchestra had vanished. Boucher, absorbed in his playing, had noted nothing of all this. As he reached the final trill be raised his foot to prepare the orchestra for the agreed cue. Then, confident both of his success and the entrance of the orchestra, he brought it down. Imagine his confusion at hearing nothing but the resounding stamp of his own foot! Horrified, he looked around and discovered the deserted desks. The audience, which had eagerly awaited this moment, broke into gales of laughter. Poor Boucher had no choice but to join in the fun.

The time had now arrived for our departure for London. As I had decided to buy my wife a new Erard harp with the improved mechanism, a *double mouvement*,[8] in London, we left our old instrument with the Vogels, to be picked up on our return journey. This was more than agreeable to the Vogels, as it guaranteed a reunion.

We arrived in London after a stormy crossing from Calais, met Ries, and settled down in the quarters that

---

[8] *A double mouvement*, or double-action harp, perfected by Erard in 1810 and permitting the intonation of a string to be altered twice by the use of pedals.

had been rented for us. On the day following I was introduced to the directors of the Philharmonic Society, who welcomed me, some in German, others in French, and we discussed the program for the first concert. I was asked to play two solos and to conduct from the concertmaster's position: I replied that I would gladly comply with the first requirement, begged, however, to be excused from the second, as my solo playing would suffer if I had to discharge both responsibilities on the same evening. Although this seemed reasonable enough to some of the gentlemen who were also soloists, much lively discussion was required before the concession was granted, as it represented a departure from local custom.

Even greater opposition was aroused by my insistence upon playing only my own compositions at this debut. In order to distinguish its program from the insipid and trivial programs of the conventional virtuoso concerts, the Philharmonic Society had made it a rule that, aside from the Mozart and Beethoven concertos, its soloists could play only what was selected for them by the directors. However, after Ries had assured them that in Germany my violin concertos were considered to be in the same class as those for which the directors had agreed that exceptions might be made, this request, too, was granted.

Thus I presented myself at the first Philharmonic concert with my *Gesangsszene* in the first half of the program and with my Solo-Quartet in E in the second, and was most well received. As composer I was particularly pleased to find that the directors now fully supported the opinions of Ries, while as violinist I was delighted to learn that old Viotti had been in the audience and had praised my playing. He had always been my model, and in my youth I had hoped to study with him.

With my London debut successfully behind me, I devoted the following days to delivering my letters of introduction. For me, with not a word of English, this was hard work, and brought me much embarrassment. Nor had anyone told me that in London it is customary to knock on the door, a gentleman distinguishing himself by rapid, repeated knocking. Following the German custom, I pulled the bell, used in London only by those who have business with the kitchen, and was at a loss to understand the astonishment of those who opened and found that I wished to be announced to the family. Since those whom I visited, and their servants, frequently spoke neither French nor German, there were some embarrassing moments.

An amusing one took place at Rothschild's,[9] to whom I brought a letter of introduction from his brother in Frankfurt and a letter of credit from Speyer. After looking at both letters, Rothschild said to me in a patronizing tone: "I see (pointing to the *Times*, which he had just been reading) that you have done well. I know nothing about music; my music is this (pointing to his purse); that is the music which they understand at the bourse." He laughed heartily at his own joke and, without inviting me to sit down, called an assistant, gave him the letter of credit, and said: "Pay the gentleman his money." He then nodded his head, and the audience was at an end. Just as I reached the door he called after me, "You may come and

[9] Nathan Mayer von Rothschild (1777–1836), third son of the founder of the famous banking concern.

dine with me some day at my country place!" Indeed, a few days later, Madame Rothschild did send me an invitation to dinner. I did not go, even though the invitation was repeated. However, the introduction to Rothschild was not in vain, for he took a box for my benefit concert.

At the home of Ries, I made the acquaintance of Erard,[10] head of the London branch of Erard Frères, and, accompanied by my wife, inspected his store of finished harps. We could not make up our minds right away about which to select, as Dorette could only determine after a good deal of playing which size suited her best and, indeed, whether she could accustom herself at all to the new mechanism. Erard put an end to this embarrassment by telling her she might have any harp she wanted for the duration of our stay in London, and, if it did not suit her, exchange it for another or give up the idea altogether. She accepted with thanks, selected an instrument and began forthwith to practice on it. Nothing went well at first. The new harp, although of the smallest size, was considerably larger than her own, and more strongly strung, requiring more strength to play. Nor did she find it easy to accustom herself to the mechanism, "a double movement," having played the simpler harp since childhood. It was soon clear that it would be months before she could play this harp in public. I decided, therefore, that she would play only in my benefit concert, to give the latter a touch of pleasing novelty.

The time was now at hand for me to conduct my first

---

[10] Sebastien Erard (1752–1831), most distinguished of the distinguished family of French instrument makers, a great contributor, not only to the modern development of the harp, but also to the piano.

Philharmonic concert, and I occasioned hardly less excitement than with my first appearance as soloist. It was still the custom in London that, in the playing of overtures and symphonies, the pianist sat at the piano with the score before him. He did not conduct, but rather read along and joined in when it suited him, which made a very bad effect. The actual conductor was the first violinist, who gave the tempo and, when things went wrong, beat time with his bow. An orchestra as large as the Philharmonic, with the musicians standing so far apart, could not achieve real precision under such a system. Despite the excellence of the individual musicians, the ensemble was much worse than that to which one was accustomed in Germany. I had decided, accordingly, that when it came my turn to conduct, I would attempt to improve matters.[11]

Fortunately, when the time came, Ries was at the piano and gladly agreed to turn the score over to me and remove himself from the proceedings. I took my place, with the score before me, at a desk especially set up in front of the orchestra, drew my baton from my pocket and gave the signal to begin. Shocked at such an innovation, some of the directors wished to protest. However, when I asked them at least to give it a try, they consented. I had conducted the symphonies and overtures on the program many times in Germany and was abundantly familiar

[11] According to Grove, "Until Spohr came there was no conductor [of the Philharmonic] as we know the term, the responsibilities being divided between the leader of the orchestra and the musician who presided at the piano." Curiously, Sir George Smart, who must have attended this concert, and who certainly would have heard of it, visited Spohr in Kassel in 1825 and wrote of the occasion: "Spohr beat time, he did not use his violin when conducting."

with them. Then I could not only set the tempi with authority, but also signal the entrances to the woodwinds and brass, giving them a degree of security they had never previously enjoyed. I also took the liberty of interrupting when things were not satisfactory, and politely but firmly making my wishes known, with Ries acting as interpreter. By this means the orchestra was prompted to extraordinary attentiveness. The visible outline of the beat contributed to security, and they all played with a fire and precision never achieved by them before.

Surprised and delighted by this success, the orchestra expressed its approval immediately after the first movement of the symphony, and there was no further opposition from the directors. Even in the choral pieces, the direction of which I entrusted to Ries, this method of giving the beat with a baton proved itself, particularly in the recitatives, and the singers expressed their satisfaction with the precision with which the orchestra accompanied them.

The success of the concert itself was even greater than I had hoped. The listeners were, to be sure, disturbed at first by the novelty, and there was a good deal of whispered comment. But when the music began, and the orchestra attacked the familiar symphony with such unwonted force and precision, prolonged applause after the first movement confirmed the favorable verdict. The victory of the baton was complete and never again was a pianist to be seen during the playing of overtures and symphonies.

A concert overture, which I had completed before my departure from Frankfurt had its first performance at this concert. As it proved very successful, the Philharmonic Society accepted it as the composition required by my contract. I kept no copy, and forgot it so completely that some years later, when compiling a thematic catalogue of my works, I could no longer remember how it went and had to omit it.

In delivering my letters in London, and on other occasions, I was repeatedly conscious of the need to have someone with me to act as interpreter. Ries finally remembered an old servant of the late Salomon[12] named Johanning, who, he thought, might meet the requirements. This fellow had retired some years before and settled down on a little property left to him by his former employer in the vicinity of London. Ries hoped that he might accept the post anyway, and summoned him to London. When he learned that his new employer was not only a German and a musician but also a violinist, as his former master had been, he accepted forthwith, leaving to me to determine his fee at the close of the season.

He came to town every morning, translated my wife's wishes for the kitchen to the landlady, and then accompanied me upon my rounds. Thanks to his long residence in London he had forgotten some of his German. His English was presumably less than classical. In any case, his interpreting led to a number of misunderstandings. For

[12] Johann Peter Salomon (1745–1815), German violinist and entrepreneur, one of the founders of the Philharmonic Society, playing a quintet by Boccherini at the first concert. His name has come down through history associated with the twelve symphonies which Haydn wrote for concerts given in London under his management in 1791 and 1794. Haydn wrote his last quartets for Salomon, and with Salomon's playing in mind.

the rest, he was a good and devoted soul, and developed a great attachment to my wife and me. Now that I was able to deliver the rest of my letters with less difficulty than before, I could find time and leisure for further composition.

My first work was a symphony (the second, in D minor, Opus 49), which I introduced at a Philharmonic concert on April 10, 1820. It found general favor at the rehearsal and real enthusiasm at the concert. This success was due in part to the excellent strings of this orchestra, to whom I had given a special opportunity to display their virtuosity in pure and precise ensemble playing. As a matter of fact, with respect to the strings, I never again heard this symphony played so well.

All the newspapers of London carried reports the next day about this new symphony, composed in their city, and outdid one another in singing its praises. Similar praise for my playing after each appearance soon spread my reputation throughout the city, and I was confronted with pupils who wished to take violin lessons from me and ladies who wished to be accompanied at the piano. As they were all prepared to pay a guinea an hour, I accepted them, feeling it a duty to my family to turn my artistic success in London to pecuniary advantage.

Thus, each day, after spending some hours at home, composing or rehearsing with my wife, I set off about London giving lessons. It was rather uphill work, for most of my pupils had neither talent nor industry, and took lessons only in order to be able to say they were pupils of Spohr. Nevertheless, I remember with pleasure certain characters who delighted me with their eccentricities and so eased my otherwise dull work.

One of these was an old, retired general, who always appeared in uniform, with all his medals, and with an unfailing military bearing. Unlike the other pupils, he came to me in my apartment, but demanded, nevertheless, only three-quarters of an hour, the custom in London being to reckon a quarter of an hour as travel time. He came every morning, excepting Sundays, precisely at noon, in his old official carriage, livried attendant carrying his violin case. With a mute greeting he would seat himself before the music stand, first pulling out his watch in order to note the exact minute on which the hour began, then laying the watch beside him. He usually brought easy duets along, mostly by Pleyel, in which I played second violin. Although his playing was in many respects quite studentlike, I soon realized that not much could be done about it, and contented myself with adapting my playing as much as possible to his. Thus, in perfect harmony with one another, we played one duet after another. As soon as three-quarters of an hour had passed, the old general would stop, even in the middle of a piece, pull out a pound note wrapped around a schilling, and lay it upon the table. Then he would take his watch, bow silently, and withdraw.

Another was an old lady who used to accompany me on the piano. She was a passionate admirer of Beethoven. There was nothing objectionable in that, but she carried her devotion to the point of playing no other music. She had scores of all of Beethoven's piano compositions as well as piano arrangements of all the orchestral works. Even her room was adorned with all the portraits of Beethoven that she had been able to find. As many of these were rather dissimilar, she required me to tell her which was the best resemblance. She had a number of souvenirs of Beethoven, brought to her from Vienna by British travelers, among them a button from his nightgown and a piece of music paper with a few pen scratches and drops of ink from his hand.

When she learned that I had been on friendly terms with Beethoven for some time, I rose quite perceptibly in her estimation and had to answer so many questions about him that on some days we hardly got around to playing. She spoke fairly fluent French and even managed a few words of German. She was not a bad pianist, and I enjoyed playing the violin and piano sonatas with her. Later on, however, she wanted to do the trios, but without cello, and even the piano concertos, with me playing the first violin and all else missing, This persuaded me that her enthusiasm for Beethoven was something of a pose and that she lacked a real understanding of the beauties of his compositions.

There was a third eccentric whom I met in the following fashion. One morning a livried servant brought me a letter, which old Johanning translated for me. "Mr. Spohr," it said, "is invited to present himself at the home of the undersigned at four o'clock precisely." Since I could not read the signature, nor learn from the servant the reason for my summons, I responded in the same laconic style: "I have business to do at the appointed time and cannot come."

Next morning the servant reappeared with a second, more politely phrased letter. It said: "The undersigned begs Mr. Spohr to honor him with a visit, and to name his own time." The servant had also been directed to place his master's carriage at my disposal for the visit. I had learned, in the meantime, that my correspondent was a famous physician and a concertgoer with a special enthusiasm for the violin. I had no further compunction about accepting, and named a time.

An elderly, friendly gentleman greeted me on the step, but as he spoke neither German nor French, we were quite incapable of communicating with one another. We stood for a few embarrassing moments, facing each other silently, until he took me by the arm and led me into a large room, the walls of which were hung with violins. Other violins had been removed from their cases and were laid out on tables. The doctor handed me a bow and pointed to one of the instruments. I suddenly realized that I was to pass judgment on the various violins, and so began to play them one after the other, and to sort them out according to their quality. It was no mean job, for there were many of them, and the old gentlemen brought them all out, down to the very last one. After about an hour I had narrowed the choice down to six, and was going through these again in order to select the very best when I became aware of a certain transfigured expression which lighted the doctor's face at the sound of one particular instrument. I gladly did him the favor of designating this violin the matador of the entire collection.

Delighted with this selection, the old gentleman brought

out a viole d'amour[13] and began to improvise upon it. I listened with pleasure, for the instrument was totally unfamiliar to me, and the doctor's playing not at all bad. Thus ended the visit to the satisfaction of both parties, and I had already taken up my hat to leave when the doctor, with a deep bow, presented me with a five-pound note. I was astonished and hardly knew what to do until it suddenly occurred to me that this was a fee for professional appraisal. I shook my head, laid the note on a table, and dashed down the steps. He followed me to the street, helped me into the carriage and, visibly excited, whispered something to the coachman. The latter passed this on to old Johanning upon our return, and he later passed it on to me. The whispered message had been: "You are driving a German who is a real gentleman. See to it that he gets home safely." Some months later, when I gave my benefit concert, the doctor ordered a ticket and left ten pounds for it!

My wife had been practicing assiduously on her new harp, but because of the wider range and the heavier strings, she found it difficult to master, and was beginning to show signs of the strain. I knew from earlier experience that nothing so eased her nerves as fresh air, and accordingly took advantage of every ray of sunshine to take short walks in Regents Park, which lay not far from our flat in Charlotte Street. On Sundays, when all music ceases in London, and one cannot even play at home without causing offense, we would make longer excursions to Hampstead, or to the more distant parks. These had the

[13] The tenor in the family of viols, predecessors of the modern violin family.

expected beneficial effect upon my wife's health and spirits. I held, however, to my earlier decision that she should not play publicly except at my concert, and turned down a number of offers made to her.

I, myself, played whenever and wherever my fee was met, and as this was not immoderately high by English standards, my name figured in almost all the concerts of the season. I could not, however, bring myself to play for money at private musicales, largely because of the shabby way in which artists were treated in those days. They were not permitted to appear among the invited company, but had to wait in a separate room until summoned to appear. Their performance completed, they had to retire forthwith. My wife and I were, ourselves, once witnesses of this ignominious treatment of London's best and most reputable artists. We had been commended to the King's brothers, the Dukes of Sussex and Clarence. As the latter was married to a German, the Princess of Meiningen, we visited this couple together. They received us most cordially, and invited us to a musicale which was to take place a few days later. We also were urged to participate. I wondered how we might avoid the distasteful separation from the other guests, and finally decided that if it were imposed upon us, we would simply turn on our heels and go home.

Accordingly, as we arrived at the ducal palace and a servant showed us to a room where the other artists were waiting, I simply had Johanning hand him my violin case, continuing up the steps, my wife on my arm, before the servant had time to recover from his astonishment. At the entrance to the salon where the invited company was assembled, I gave my name to the servant posted there. When he hesitated to open the door, I made a gesture as if to open it myself. At this the servant opened the door and announced us. The Duchess, mindful of German custom, arose from her seat, approached my wife, and led her to the circle of ladies. The Duke, too, welcomed me cordially and introduced me to the gentlemen. I reckoned that I had brought it all off successfully, but soon noticed that the servants continued to regard me as an intruder, refusing to serve me tea or any of the other refreshments. The Duke must have noticed this, for I saw him summon the major-domo and whisper a few words in his ear, after which I, too, was served.

When time came for the concert to begin the major-domo had the artists summoned one after the other, according to their place on the program. They appeared, notes or instrument in hand, greeted the company with a deep obeisance—acknowledged by no one, as far as I could see, except the Duchess—and played or sang whatever it was that they were supposed to sing or play. It was the elite of the most distinguished artists and virtuosos of London, and their performances were almost all very beautiful. They seemed lost upon the illustrious audience, for conversation continued without a moment's interruption. Only the appearance of a particularly beloved female singer brought some quiet to the scene, and one heard a few softly articulated "Bravos," which she promptly acknowledged with a grateful bow. I was much angered by this indignity to the art, and even more by the artists who accepted such treatment. I had a great desire not to play, and, when my turn came, delayed so long that the Duke himself, probably at a sign from the Duchess, entreated me to do so.

Not until then did I summon a servant to bring up my violin case. Instrument in hand, I began to play, dispensing with the preliminary obeisance. The foregoing must have attracted the attention of the company, for there was complete silence in the room while I played. When I had finished, the Duke and Duchess applauded, the others joining in. The concert came to an end soon afterwards, and the artists withdrew. If our having joined the company upon arrival had caused a sensation, the sensation was multiplied when we stayed to supper and were most attentively treated by our ducal hosts. For this courteous treatment, unexampled according to the English customs of that time, we could thank the circumstance that the Duchess had, in her parental household, been witness to the gracious attention repeatedly accorded me at the court at Meiningen.

Among those who invited me to participate as soloist in their concerts was Sir George Smart, one of the directors of the Philharmonic Society. He gave a series of subscription concerts during the season, calling them "spiritual," although they contained much that was profane. I played in two of them, as a result of which he took over the arrangements for my benefit concert. This was an undertaking taxing enough for the native initiate. Had I done it myself, it would have taken possibly six weeks of time which I could well invest more advantageously.

The concert took place on June 18, and was one of the most brilliant and well-attended of the entire season. Almost all of the personages to whom we had been commended, including the Dukes of Sussex and Clarence, took boxes or stalls, and a number of these illustrious gentlemen donated substantial sums for them. A great proportion of the subscribers to the Philharmonic Society's concerts retained their seats, and since the cheapest seat was a guinea, and the hall accommodated a thousand persons, the income was considerable. Moreover, the expenses, normally very high in London, were reduced by the refusal of a number of the members of the Philharmonic, as a gesture to me, to accept a fee. The hall, in accordance with the terms of my contract, was free. All the singers, however, had to be paid, and I still remember paying Mrs. Salmon,[14] the most popular of the singers in London at that time, thirty pounds for a single aria. A concert without her had no proper standing. She required, moreover, that her appearance be delayed until toward the end of the concert, as she had also to sing the same evening in the City, six miles away.

I must mention here one expense connected with the concert, if only because, like many other oddities of those days, it no longer exists. It was the custom for the concert-giver to serve his audience refreshments gratis during the intermission between the first and second halves of the program. They were served at a buffet in an adjoining room by a caterer according to a sum agreed upon in advance between the concert-giver and the caterer. In my case this sum was ten pounds sterling. If the audience was composed for the most part of people from the upper classes, among whom it was considered bad form to par-

[14] Mrs. Salmon, *née* Eliza Munday (1787–1849), the most fashionable singer in London between 1815 and 1825.

take, the caterer made a tidy profit. If, on the other hand, the audience was large and mixed, and the weather warm, he could count upon a considerable loss.

Never was the caterer better served than at my concert. It took place the day Queen Charlotte returned from Italy to appear before Parliament to defend herself against her husband's charge of infidelity. All London took sides, the lower and middle classes standing solidly behind the Queen. The entire city was in a state of great excitement, and it was lucky for me that all the tickets for my concert had already been sold, for otherwise I would have stood to lose a great deal. The placards announcing my concert were soon pasted over with larger ones proclaiming, in the name of the people, a general illumination of the city to celebrate the Queen's return. Johanning brought news that the people were threatening to smash in the windows of any house that failed to participate. As the police and military forces available were inadequate to defend the government buildings against the threatened excesses of the mob, the partisans of the King, who could hardly participate in the illumination, had no choice but to take what came. The most that they could do in the way of defense was to board up as many of their windows as the short time permitted. There was hammering all day, particularly in nearby Portland Place where the nobility had their town houses.

While we stayed at home, preparing for the concert, great crowds surged through the streets to greet the Queen. Fortunately, their destination was the City, so that by evening it was quiet in the West End. We found the streets emptier than usual as we drove to the concert hall at seven-thirty, and there were no obstacles in our path. But everywhere we noted that people were hastily preparing for the illumination so that, with nightfall, the will of the sovereign people could be accommodated. My wife, agitated anyway before her first public appearance with the new harp, was much concerned about what might happen, and I was deeply troubled that her nervous excitement might adversely affect her playing. And so I tried to reassure her, not without some success.

The hall filled little by little, and the concert began. I can give the program in its entirety, as Sir George Smart presented me with a copy of the sheet handed to the listeners as they arrived:

NEW ARGYLL ROOMS[15]
MR. SPOHR'S CONCERT
Thursday, June 18, 1820

PART I

Grand Sinfonia (M.S.)	Spohr
Air, Mr. T. Welch "Revenge, revenge, Timotheus cries"	Handel
Grand Duetto (M.S.) Harp and Violin Mad. Spohr and Mr. Spohr	Spohr
Aria, Miss Goodall "Una Voce al cor mi parla" Clarinet Obligato Mr. Wellman	Paer
Sestetto for Pianoforte, two Violins, Viola, Violoncello and Contrabasso, Messrs.: Ries, Watts, Wagstaff, R. Ashley, Lindley and Dragonetti	Ries

[15] They were the first home of the Philharmonic Society, on the east side of Regent Street, at the northwest corner of Little Argyll Street. The building was destroyed by fire in 1830.

Irish Melodies (M.S.) with Variations for the
 Violin, Mr. Spohr (composed expressly for
 this occasion)   Spohr

PART II

Nonetto for Violin, Viola, Violoncello, Contrabasso,
 Flute, Oboe, Clarinet, Horn and Bassoon,
 Messrs. Spohr, Lindley, Dragonetti, Ireland
 Griesbach, Wellman, Arnull and Holmes[16]   Spohr
Scena, Mrs. Salmon, "Fellon, la Pena arrai"   Rossini
Rondo for Violin, Mr. Spohr   Spohr
Aria, Mr. Vaughan, "Rend'il sereno"   Handel
Overture   Spohr
        Leader of the Band – – – Mr. Spohr
        At the Pianoforte – – – Sir George Smart

The new symphony, already familiar to the orchestra,
but again carefully rehearsed, was played in a most masterly fashion, and excited even livelier applause than at
the first performance. During the following aria I tuned
my wife's harp offstage and did my best to encourage her.
Then I conducted her to the stage and we took our places
to begin the duet. An expectant quiet had already de-
scended upon the auditorium when suddenly there was
frightful shouting in the street, followed by a cannonade

[16] The attentive reader will note that only eight players are named.
Since most of those listed can be identified, and since these identifica-
tions indicate that the names are listed according to the order of the
instruments, and since Spohr can be identified as the violinist, Lindley
as the cellist, and Dragonetti as the bassist, it follows that the violist
is missing. From the listing of the participants in the preceding sextet,
it is similarly possible to identify R. Ashley as the violist. Hence, it is a
reasonable assumption that R. Ashley is the missing member.

of cobblestones against the unlighted windows of the adjoining room. At the sound of the shattering glass the ladies sprang from their seats, and there was an indescribable scene of excitement and confusion. Attendants hurried to light the gas lamps in the adjoining room in order to forestall a second salvo. The maneuver succeeded. There was an exultant shout from the mob at this evidence of success, and it moved on. Little by little order was restored, but it was still some time before the audience was again seated and sufficiently composed to permit the concert to continue.

I was afraid, of course, that the shock and the long wait might have seriously disconcerted my wife, and I awaited her first chords with some anxiety. When these sounded in their usual strength I was able to relax and devote my attention to our ensemble. This ensemble had always attracted favorable attention in Germany, and the English public found it no less pleasing. The applause increased from movement to movement of the duet, and at the end grew into an ovation. As we left the stage, highly pleased with our success, we little thought that this was to be the last time that Dorette would play the harp. But of that, more later!

As to the other numbers of the program in which I, myself, participated, I was especially pleased by the reception accorded the Nonet. I had already played it once with the same artists at a Philharmonic concert, and had been urged to repeat it at my own concert. The precision of our ensemble this time was even more nearly perfect, and its success was assured. The Irish Songs were also well received.

Thus, despite the disruptive intermezzo, the concert ended to the satisfaction of all concerned. Because of the destruction in the adjoining room, the intermission and the promenade could not take place, and the caterer had a clean profit of ten pounds, excepting only what was damaged on the buffet by the hail of stones.

I come now to a sad period in my life. As a result of the strain of attempting to master the new harp and the tensions of the concert, my wife felt so exhausted and ailing that I feared another nervous breakdown. It was high time to make a serious decision. Following her breakdown in Darmstadt, I had tried to persuade her to give up her nerve-racking instrument, but when I saw how badly she took the proposal, I said no more about it. She was too thoroughly an artist by nature, and was too devoted to the instrument which had brought her so many triumphs, to be able to abandon it easily. Moreover, it pleased her that, through her talent, she could contribute to the family's earnings. Now, however, herself convinced that her strength was inadequate for the new instrument, and aware that the old instrument would never again fully satisfy her, she was more reasonably disposed to my renewed proposal, particularly when I pointed out that she could continue to participate in my concerts as pianist. This was most reassuring, although it was plain to her that she would never enjoy such successes on the piano as on the harp, on which, in Germany, at least, she had no equal. I promised, moreover, to write brilliant concerto movements for her, in order to add the charm of novelty to her appearances. It was, in any case, high time that I tried my hand at piano composition, and so, before our departure from London, I wrote the first movement of my Piano Quintet, Opus 52. I returned the harp to Erard, if only to remove it from her sight. Upon learning that my wife had to give up the instrument because of her health, he took it back, refusing to accept any rental fee for its use. He added gallantly that it had only now achieved its full value, having been broken in by such a famous artist and played by her in her last public appearance. I now again took daily walks with my wife in the open air and noted with pleasure and relief that, little by little, she recovered her strength. The prospect of being reunited with her children certainly contributed to her convalescence. I, too, was eager to be with the family once more, and as soon as the last Philharmonic concert was over, we made plans to depart.

When I broke the news to poor old Johanning, his eyes filled with tears. He had become so fond of us that he refused at first to accept any compensation for the services he had rendered. When I pressed him he finally agreed to accept a salary at a figure set by me, although only against one condition, from which I was not to attempt to dissuade him. I told him to name it, but it was some time before I could get it out of him. Finally, in great embarrassment, he invited me and my wife to do him the honor of having our last dinner in London at his home. When we accepted without hesitation, his whole face became transfigured, and he could not find the words to express his gratitude.

He appeared on the appointed day spick and span in his late master's formal clothes, with white silk stockings and powdered hair. At the door was a four-seater carriage which was to bring us to his home and in which we found a famous artist, the most intimate friend of his late master, who had also been invited. When we were seated, however, Johanning refused to take the fourth seat, insisting that it was unfitting, despite my protests that he was no longer my servant but now my host. He could not be swayed, and took his accustomed place beside the coachman. During the ride, our new companion regaled us with stories of Johanning's devotion to his former master. Among other things he said that Johanning had spent the better part of his inheritance to build a monument to his master in Westminster Abbey. We were overcome with new respect and admiration for the man who had so recently been our servant.

Upon our arrival he opened the carriage door and conducted us on to his property. It consisted of a small house and an adjoining small garden. Everything was neat and clean. First he accompanied us up some steps and into the drawing room, not forgetting to call our attention to a bell rope next to the fireplace. He even pulled it, although no servant could respond, he and his wife being their own servants. We then took a short stroll in the garden and were conducted at last to the dining room, where we found the table set for three persons. Johanning again refused to sit with us, for the excellent reason, this time, that had he done so there would have been nobody to serve us. He brought the food from the kitchen and served us, his face a picture of joy. The excellent dinner was presented on the elegant service of his late master. We doubtless had the latter to thank for the fine Rhine wine, too. The dessert, strawberries and cherries, came from the garden.

After the dinner, we were shown to the drawing room, where we met Mrs. Johanning, who had hitherto been preoccupied with the preparation of the meal. She, too, was in her Sunday best. Now, at last, after much hesitation, the worthy old couple consented to take places at the table with us and share the coffee. Johanning was beside himself with pride and pleasure, as he translated for his wife the words of praise we expended on her cooking. Toward evening the carriage drove before the door to take us home. We said our farewells, much moved. Johanning could not be dissuaded from climbing up next to the coachman to accompany us home and open the carriage door for us upon our arrival. Indeed, next morning he was there again to offer any assistance that might be required. At the carriage station we found many friends and acquaintances gathered to see us off.

INTERVAL

THE SPOHRS RETURNED TO GERMANY and settled down for a time with the family in Gandersheim. Here, Spohr completed the Quintet for Piano, Flute, Clarinet, Horn, and Bassoon which he had begun in London as a vehicle for his wife. With this as a stimulus, Dorette went to work with enthusiasm and persistence and seems to have managed the transition from the harp remarkably well. She introduced the new work at a concert which they gave in Frankfurt on their way to Paris in the fall of 1820. Spohr described their stay in Paris in the following series of letters to the *Musikalische Zeitung* in Leipzig.

IX

JOURNEY TO PARIS

(1820–21)

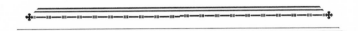

December 17, 1820

I HOPE, MY FRIEND, that you will appreciate the fact that I write to you only eight days after our arrival in Paris, at a time, indeed, when I am so overwhelmed by so much that is new that I shall find it difficult to sort things out.

My heart beat fast as I drove through the Paris gate. The thought that I would soon have the pleasure of meeting artists whose works had been known to me since my earliest childhood was tremendously exciting. Indeed, I recalled the time when, as a young boy, Cherubini[1] had been my idol. Back in Braunschweig I had learned to know his works even before those of Mozart. I remembered the evening when I heard *Les Deux Journées* for the first time, how, completely intoxicated by the powerful impression this work had made upon me, I got hold of a

[1] Cherubini was then professor of composition at the Paris *Conservatoire*, a position he was to hold until 1841.

score and stayed up all night with it, and how it was primarily this opera that gave me the first impulse to compose. The creator of this work and many other men whose music had had a decisive influence upon my own development as composer and violinist would soon be before me in the flesh.

Thus, almost before we had a roof over our heads, I made it my business to start looking up various famous artists. All received me in a most friendly manner, and with many of them I subsequently developed a close personal relationship. Of Cherubini it was said that he was normally very reserved with strangers, at least at the outset. I did not find him so. Although I brought no letter of introduction, he greeted me most cordially, and urged me to repeat my visit as often as I wished.

On the evening of our arrival Kreutzer took us to the Grand Opera, where a ballet of his, *Le Carnaval de Venise*, was given. With both the singers and the dancers of the Grand Opera, one noticed that they were accustomed to working in a larger frame; in their present surroundings,[2] much smaller than the deserted Opera House, what they did seemed too obvious and overdone. Many of the big operas, particularly Gluck's, cannot be given, as there is not even space for the orchestra. Thus, everyone is looking forward eagerly to the completion of the new house, which, as hard as they are working on it, will hardly be finished before midsummer.

Before the ballet they gave the opera, *Le Devin du Vil-*

[2] It is not clear what or where this building was. The building referred to as being under construction was the Salle Favart, where the company opened on May 3, 1821. The present Paris Opera dates from 1875.

lage, text and music by Rousseau. What is one to say of the French, who, along with the many new operas with which their repertoire has been enriched in the past twenty years, continue to play also the very oldest? Is it a sign of progressive, cultivated taste when the oldest operas of Grétry,[3] with all their harmonic poverty and incorrectness, are greeted with the same, if not greater enthusiasm than the masterpieces of Cherubini and Méhul?[4] I doubt it. How long ago it seems that the operas of Hiller,[5] Dittersdorf,[6] and others of that time vanished from our repertoire, although their musical substance is considerably superior to most of Grétry's. To be sure, it is depressing that with us only what is new can make any headway, however dull and faulty, while many excellent older works are put aside and forgotten. And yet one may score it to the Germans' credit that at least the Mozart operas constitute an exception, and that for more than thirty years now they have continued in the repertoire of every German theater. This proves that the German nation has finally become permeated with the incomparable perfection of these masterpieces and cannot be seduced by the sweet musical poison being wafted in our direction from south of the Alps.

[3] André Ernest Modeste Grétry (1741–1813), one of the great classical composers of French *opéra-comique*. It is he of whom it was said, because of the thinness of his harmony, that one could drive a coach-and-four between the bass and the first fiddle.

[4] Étienne Nicolas Méhul (1763–1817), leading French opera composer of his generation. *Joseph* was his most famous work.

[5] Johann Adam Hiller (1728–1804), who, as a composer of Singspiele, was one of the founding fathers of indigenous German opera.

[6] Karl Ditters von Dittersdorf (1739–99), prolific Austrian composer, his twenty-eight operettas constituting an early foundation for German indigenous musical theater.

The orchestra of the Grand Opera, as compared with the other orchestras, has the greatest number of famous and distinguished artists, but is said to be inferior to that of the Italian Opera in respect of ensemble. About this I cannot judge, not having heard the other orchestra. In Kreutzer's ballet, which was played with notable precision, I was particularly taken with the masterly oboe solo of Voigt. This artist has succeeded in achieving an absolute evenness in tone and intonation over the impressive range from C to F above the staff, an enterprise on which most oboists would come to grief. His playing is, moreover, a model of taste and charm.

I was less favorably impressed by the Grand Opera a few days ago when they gave *Les Mystères d'Isis.*[7] Mozart's admirers are only too justified in their complaints about this adaptation of Mozart's wonderful *The Magic Flute*, which, when first introduced, was renamed by the French themselves *Les Misères d'Isis.* Even more shameful is the fact that it was Germans who committed this outrage upon the immortal master. Nothing has been left untouched except the overture. Everything else has been tumbled together, altered, and emasculated. The opera begins with the final chorus of *The Magic Flute;* then comes the March from *La Clemenza di Tito*, then this and that from various other Mozart operas, not to mention an excerpt from a Haydn symphony, along with recitatives from Lachnith's own factory.

Worst of all is the fact that the adapters have provided

---

[7] *Les Mystères d'Isis*, an arrangement of *The Magic Flute* by Ludwig Wenzel Lachnith (1746–1820), first introduced at the Grand Opera, August 23, 1801. It led to Lachnith's being referred to as *"le dérangeur."*

serious texts for amiable, even comical episodes in *The Magic Flute*, which makes of the music a parody of the text and the situation. Papagena, for example, sings the character-revealing aria of the Moor, *"Alles fuehlt der Liebe Freuden."* The lovely trio of the Three Boys, *"Seid uns zum zweitenmal willkommen,"* is sung by the Three Ladies. The duet, *"Bie Maennern, welche Liebe fuehlen,"* has become a trio. Even worse are the actual alterations in the score. In the aria, *"In diesen heiligen Hallen,"* for example, at the passage, *"So wandelt er an Freundes Hand,"* the imitative figure in the bass, not only essential to the harmony, but also illustrative of the text, is missing entirely. The basses merely hit the B a few times. You can imagine how dreary and cold this passage sounds, which in Germany has so often been singled out for special admiration! Moreover, in the songs of the Three Ladies, where Mozart reinforced the third voice only with the violins, the adapters have added cellos and double basses, so that the bass notes, in these tender, mostly only three-voiced passages, sound in three separate octaves, which, for the cultivated ear, is sheerly intolerable. It is only just to say for the French that they have always been against this vandalism (the extent of which they can hardly grasp, as they are unfamiliar with the original); but how is it that, nevertheless, these *mystères* have held on in the repertoire for close to twenty years, particularly since, as I can confirm from day-to-day experience, the public rules here and can impose its will whenever it wishes to?

For me, as a German, the performance, too, was unsatisfactory. Even the overture did not go as well as one might have expected from such fine artists. It was taken too fast, and toward the end this evil was compounded, with the result that violinists, where they should have been playing sixteenths, had to be content with eighths. The singers of the Grand Opera, as fine as they may be in declamation, are ill-suited to the tender songs of *The Magic Flute*. They sing with a roughness that destroys any hint of gentle sentiment. The staging is decent, but not so splendid as I had expected it to be.

Yesterday we paid a third visit to the Grand Opera and saw *Clari*, a major ballet in three acts with music by Kreutzer. As little as I like ballet, I cannot deny that the Paris Ballet can be pleasantly diverting, at least for a while, until the monotony of the mimic movements and the even greater monotony of the dances becomes tiresome. Even when it is as well done as it is here, I find pantomime, as compared to the spoken drama, on a par with a draft as compared to a finished drawing, requiring, as it does, a printed explanation. One may deck it out as one will (here with the splendor of the sets and costumes), it remains a mere outline without inner life. Similarly I would equate the theater, as against opera, with a drawing as against a painting. Only through song does the poem receive its color and shade, and only song, supported by the communicative power of harmony, can express the intangible, intuitively felt surgings of the spirit, which even speech can no more than suggest.

December 31, 1820

Fourteen very pleasant days have passed since I sent off my last letter, and we have seen and heard many beautiful things. In telling you about it, however, I must restrict myself to that which is immediately concerned with my art. I have now presented myself as composer and violinist to professionals and amateurs, connoisseurs and laymen. I played first for Baudiot,[8] first cellist of the Royal Orchestra. Next day I played for Kreutzer, and since then I have appeared at three musicales. On the first two occasions the listeners were mostly professionals. Kreutzer had invited almost all the most distinguished composers and violinists of Paris. I played a number of my quartets and quintets, and at Kreutzer's, the Nonet. The composers all said nice things about my compositions, the violinists about my playing. Among the latter were Viotti, the two Kreutzers, Baillot,[9] Lafont, Habeneck,[10] Fontaine, Guerin, and many others whose names are not familiar in Germany. You can see from this what was at stake. I had to do my best if I were not to let my countrymen down. The Nonet had to be repeated. I had been sufficiently impressed by the finish with which the participants had played it at sight the first time. The repetition pleased me even more, for they had already penetrated into the inner spirit of the work.

The young pianist, Herz,[11] of whom you will have read

[8] Charles Nicolas Baudiot (1773–1849), cellist, professor at the Paris *Conservatoire*, and member of the Court Orchestra.

[9] Pierre Marie François de Sales Baillot (1771–1842), at that time concertmaster of the orchestra of the Grand Opera. He is considered to have been the last of the violinists of the French or pre-Paganini classical school.

[10] François Antoine Habeneck (1781–1849), pupil of Baillot and an excellent violinist, but better known as the outstanding French conductor of his generation. He introduced the Beethoven symphonies to Paris.

a good deal in the musical journals, played twice that evening, first some variations of his own, then Moscheles' famous variations on the "Alexander March." The extraordinary virtuosity of this young man is truly astonishing, and yet with him, as with most of the young artists whom I have heard here, technical proficiency seems to take priority over interpretive substance. Otherwise, in such a cultivated company, he would have offered something more substantial than these mere technical displays. It is most remarkable here how everyone, old and young alike, strives for mechanical brilliance, and how players, in whom there may well be the prerequisites for better things, spend years and all their energy on a single piece of worthless music in order finally to parade it before the public. That this procedure is deadly for the spirit, and that nothing better will come of such people, goes without saying.

Thus it is that one rarely hears in musical circles here a serious, substantial piece of music, such as a quartet or quintet by one of our great masters; everyone rides his war horse; there is nothing but a succession of *airs variés*, *rondos favoris*, nocturnes, and similar trifles. The singers content themselves with romances and little duets, and no matter how bad the music, the success is certain if only they are fluently and sweetly sung. Poorly equipped with such trifles, I find myself rather isolated with my serious German music, and often have the feeling of speaking to people who do not understand my language. Frequent-

11 Heinrich Herz (1803–88), better known in Paris, where he spent most of his life, as Henri Herz. Spohr's judgment of his playing was shared by Schumann.

ly, when someone who praises my playing extends his praise to my compositions, the pleasure is spoiled when I hear the same person express a similarly high opinion of some miserable triviality. It is the same in the theaters. The crowd that sets the tone cannot distinguish between good and bad. It hears *Le Jugement de Midas*[12] with the same delight as *Les Deux Journées*"[13] or *Joseph*. One need not be here very long to share the view of many that the French are an unmusical people. Even the artists here subscribe to this opinion, and tell me, when I speak of Germany in this connection: "Yes, in Germany music is loved and understood. That is not the case here." This explains why it is that in Paris beautiful music cannot save a bad libretto, whereas a good libretto can survive a miserable score.

These circumstances have left me with no desire to write for any of the local theaters, an idea that was formerly very tempting. Firstly, I would have to begin from the beginning like a young composer, since, aside from a few violin pieces, my works are hardly known here. Secondly, I would have to contend with a thousand intrigues launched against me as a foreigner. Finally, and most important, I could not be sure of success even if I wrote a good score, since success here, as I have said, depends almost solely upon the play. One may see this confirmed in the reviews of new operas in the Paris journals, where columns are devoted to the text and only a few words to the music.

Indeed, if it were not so lucrative to write for the Paris

[12] *Le Jugement de Midas*, by Grétry.
[13] *Les Deux Journées*, by Cherubini.

theater, composers would long since have given up in disgust. But since a successful opera means profits continuing over a lifetime, new works appear almost every day. Composers and poets seek constantly for new effects. They fill the journals with their plans and projects. On the evening of the *première* they engage a reliable claque. All this is designed to secure for the new work a brilliant reception and enough repetition to produce a handsome income. If there were half as much to be earned in Germany from a new opera, we would soon be as rich in gifted composers for the theater as we are now in instrumental composers, and our stages would no longer suffer from that dependency on imports which now does so little credit to the artistic cultivation of the German people.

Now, after three weeks in Paris, we have made several visits to all the Parisian theaters, and I am doubly glad that our engagements for afternoons and evenings have mounted to a point where, in the next two weeks, we shall have few evenings free for the theater.

About the *Théâtre Français*, the Odeón, and the four small theaters I shall tell you nothing, as they offer nothing of sufficient musical quality to make it worth the telling. In the first two one hears only *entr'actes*, and in the other four almost nothing but vaudeville.[14] Thanks be

14 As used here the word refers to a type of variety show or revue featuring popular songs, doubtless more distinguished for their wit than their musical substance. Originally the word referred to a type of topical popular song, but in time it came to be associated with shows featuring such songs. According to Grove: "The rage for vaudevilles gave rise to pieces entirely in verse and parodies of operas, and largely contributed to the creation of the opéra-comique. To distinguish between these different classes of pieces the name '*comédies à*

to Apollo and the Muses that nothing of this kind has been transplanted in other countries. That vaudevilles are so popular here that four theaters give nothing else is the most compelling evidence that the French are unmusical; for the sacred art of music can hardly ever have been, anywhere or at any time, so abused as in these songs that are neither sung nor spoken and which represent a flagrant contradiction of the written melody and the accompanying harmony. All Frenchmen of any taste at all are agreed that the vaudevilles, formerly confined to a single theater, are, through their multiplication, increasingly stifling all sense for true music and exercising a pernicious influence on cultural growth. We have visited each of these theaters once, in order to make the acquaintance of the famous comedians, but have in no case been tempted to return. Listening to such bad music is too great a price to pay for the pleasure which these artists, through their wit and inexhaustible spirit, do unquestionably provide. I was much impressed by the skill with which the orchestras stay with the singers, who happily disregard both notes and measure. But it is their most notable accomplishment. In all other respects they are rather mediocre.

We have visited the Italian Opera several times and have had much artistic pleasure there. Yesterday, at long last, we saw *Don Giovanni*, which had been absent from the repertoire for some time. The house was packed, and half an hour before the curtain there was not a seat to be had. I was tempted to think that the Parisians had finally

---

ariettes' was given to what are now called *opéras-comiques*, and the others became successively '*pièces en vaudeville*,' '*Comédies melées de vaudevilles*,' then '*comédies vaudevilles*' and finally '*vaudevilles*.' "

grasped the classical excellence of the work, and were storming the theater in order to enjoy them. When I noticed how the loveliest numbers, the first duet, the quartet, the great sextet, and others made little impression, I changed my mind. Only two numbers prompted much applause, and it was expended on the singers rather than the composer.

These two numbers, each of which had to be repeated, were the duet between Don Giovanni and Zerlina, "*La ci darem la mano*" and Don Giovanni's Champagne aria. The first was transposed a half-tone up, to B flat, and the latter raised a whole tone, both because of the weakness of Herr García's[15] lower register. Madame Fodor-Mainville,[16] apparently well aware that Zerlina's arias would please the Parisians more than those of Donna Elvira, wisely chose this role for herself. Her success vindicated her judgment. What mattered it to her that the opera was improperly cast, if she thereby earned the greatest applause? The connoisseur, however, can forgive her only if he forgets that this is the part of a peasant girl, and if he puts aside any thought of realistic casting. In fact, Madame Fodor-Mainville decked out the simple arias of her part with a great array of pompous embellishments. She did them well, to be sure, but they are doubly

[15] Manuel García (1775–1832), famous Spanish singer (tenor), composer, and voice teacher, now remembered chiefly as father and teacher of his own two daughters, Maria Malibran and Pauline Viardot, and his son, Manuel, the most famous singing teacher of the nineteenth century. It was for Manuel García, Sr., that Rossini wrote the role of Almaviva in *The Barber of Seville*. Although García was a tenor, *Don Giovanni* was long one of his most successful parts.

[16] Josephine Fodor-Mainville (1789–1870), a celebrated singer then in her prime. Zerlina and Rosina were among her best parts.

out of place here, first because they are inappropriate to Mozart's music, secondly because they are inappropriate to the character of Zerlina. Aside from this, it was an unusual pleasure to find this part so strongly cast. In Germany it falls too often to third-rate singers.

García, as Don Giovanni provided rather too much of a good thing. At every conceivable opportunity he is ready with a lengthy embellishment. These were most disturbing in the Serenade, where the figurations of the mandolin accompaniment rule out even the simplest ornament. He pays no attention to them, but throws in ornaments all over the place, even slowing the tempo to make room for them. His singing of the Champagne aria, on the other hand, was quite incomparable, and I confess never to have heard it done so well. Here the Italian text stands him in good stead. Unlike our German singers, who usually run out of breath in this aria, he gained in strength as he went along, right up to the end.

The other roles were more or less satisfactorily cast, none of them badly, and one must be thankful to them all for having done their best to do credit to the work. The performance as a whole was also quite satisfactory if one forgets the high standards one expects from such a theater. To a German it is clear that these singers, who sing only Italian music, particularly Rossini, with the utmost perfection, cannot execute Mozart with comparable excellence. The soft, sweet style so appropriate to Rossini, dilutes the energetic character which belongs to *Don Giovanni* even more than to other Mozart operas.

The orchestra, rated by Parisians the best in the world,

had some bad moments. The winds failed conspicuously on two occasions, and several times things got so out of hand that the director had to resort to beating time. I am more convinced than ever that a theater orchestra, be it ever so good, can only be directed by continuous time-beating, if only because the outer extremities of the orchestra are too far apart. Certainly it is not sufficient to attempt to mark time as Grasset[17] did, by movements of his body and his violin. It should be added that this orchestra is justly famous for its discretion in the accompanying of the singers. In this respect it could serve as a model for the other Paris orchestras, and many others, too.

The chorus was also excellent, and made a wonderful effect in the final allegro of the first finale. But why here, as almost everywhere else, should this allegro be taken so immoderately fast? Cannot the director see that this diminishes rather than strengthens the effect, that the triplet figures of the violins, which first animate the ensemble, cannot be heard at this speed, and that in the end, instead of a living whole, only skeletal outlines can be heard?

When one hears such a beautiful work thus disfigured by false tempi, one wonders again if it is not time to put tempo designation into general use, either by the Maelzel or by the Weber[18] method, or, preferably, both. Of

---

[17] Jean-Jacques Grasset (c.1769–1839), for many years professor of violin at the *Conservatoire* and concertmaster at the Italian Opera.

[18] The reference is to Johann Nepomuk Maelzel (1772–1838) and Gottfried Weber (1779–1839), along with Dietrich Nikolaus Winkel (c.1780–1826), the outstanding figures in the development of the metronome. Maelzel established the first metronome factory in Paris in 1816.

course, the conductors would have to allow themselves to be governed by them instead of following their own interests as at present!

January 12, 1821

It is with a sense of considerable relief that I report, my dear friend, a successful public debut. It is always a risky business for a foreign violinist to appear in Paris, as the Parisians are possessed with the mad conceit that they have the best violinists in the world, and regard it as a sort of arrogance when a stranger considers himself qualified to compete with them.

And so I am quite pleased with the brilliant reception accorded me day before yesterday, and the more so since not more than a dozen in the audience were personal friends, and I had purchased no claque. But I had prepared myself very carefully, and was admirably supported by the accompanying orchestra under the direction of Habeneck. Nor was I the least bit nervous, as I usually am before a first appearance in a foreign country, and as I certainly was in London. The explanation is probably that I had played for just about all the distinguished artists here prior to my public debut, whereas in London I had to appear at a Philharmonic concert eight days after my arrival and without having played privately for anyone.

Of my own compositions I offered the overture to *Alruna*, the newest Violin Concerto, and the Potpourri on the duet from *Don Giovanni*. There was also a cavatina by Rossini, sung by Demoiselle Cinti,[19] and a duet, also

[19] Laure Cinti-Damoreau (1801–63), who became very celebrated in later years. Rossini wrote for her the principal female parts of

by Rossini, sung by Bordogni[20] and Levasseur. We had played the overture through three times at rehearsal, and it went well, although not quite as well as the last time at rehearsal, and was well received. In the concerto and also in the Potpourri, the winds failed to come in a couple of times, probably due to the usual French negligence in counting measures. But not much damage was done. The approval of the audience, as expressed in applause and shouts of "Bravo!" was unmistakable. The critics have been less friendly, and I must tell you why.

These gentlemen are accustomed to have every artist, resident or stranger, call upon them before a public appearance, beg their favor, and present them with free tickets. Visiting artists, in order to avoid these unpleasant calls, usually present their compliments in writing, enclosing free tickets with their request for favorable attention. Sometimes they arrange to have some family, to whom they have a letter of introduction, invite the critics to lunch, where the artist can, under more comfortable circumstances, make known to them what he would like to have written about him before and after the concert. This may happen here and there in Germany, but I doubt that criticism can be anywhere so venal as here. I have been assured that the finest artists of the *Théâtre Français* pay considerable sums annually to keep these gentlemen well disposed, and that the latter know no better way out of their financial difficulties than to attack some well-

The *Siege of Corinth* and *Moise*, and Auber wrote *Domino Noir* for her.

[20] Giulio Marco Bordogni (1788–1856), tenor and pupil of Simone Mayr, later a famous teacher.

known artist until he sees the light and pays his tribute. How such venal criticism can be taken seriously is more than I can understand. Enough! I did not make these supplicant calls because I felt them to be beneath the dignity of a German artist, and thought that the worst that could come of it would be that the critics would simply stay away. About this I was wrong. They came, and they have written, some of them in terms of unstinted praise, most of them, however, with a large "but," designed to qualify whatever praise they may have been moved to give. In all of these reviews there is a conspicuous admixture of smug French vanity. All begin by pointing out the superiority of their own artists and their own cultivation. They point out that a nation which has produced Baillot, Lafont, and Habeneck has no call to envy any other nation its violinists, and that, if nevertheless, the playing of a foreign violinist has excited enthusiasm, this is no more than a demonstration of French hospitality. One critic has written: *"M. Spohr comme exécutant est un homme de mérite; il a deux qualités rares et précieuses, la pureté et la justesse,"* and closes as a true Frenchman with the phrase, *"s'il reste quelque temps à Paris, il pourra perfectionner son goût et retourner ensuite, former celui des bons Allemands."* If the good man could only know what the *"bons Allemands"* think of French artistic taste!

This ludicrous vanity of the Parisians is reflected in their conversation. When this or that artist plays they ask: "Now, have you anything to compare with that in Germany?" And when they introduce an artist to a foreigner, they never refer to him as the best in Paris, but always as the best in the world, although no nation is less aware of the cultural possessions of other nations than the French, which is probably just as well, their vanity being what it is.

You may have wondered why I have written nothing about the music in the Court Chapel. I have held off intentionally, until I could have heard some of Cherubini's masses. Lesueur[21] and Cherubini, the two musical directors of the Court Chapel, alternate every three months in the directorship. We arrived during the directorship of Lesueur, Cherubini's beginning in January. The directors do not themselves conduct the music, but rather preside in court dress at the head of the choir, without actually taking part in the performance. The actual musical director is Plantade.[22] Kreutzer is leader of the first violins, and Baillot, of the second violins. The orchestra is composed of the best artists of Paris, the choir strong and good. There are one or two rehearsals for each mass, and under Plantade's secure and spirited direction, all goes well.

Although I was prepared to hear music stylistically quite different from what we call churchly, I was still astonished by the brilliant theatrical style of a mass by Plantade which we heard during our first visit to the chapel on December 17. There was not the slightest trace of a churchly style, no canonic voice-leading, much less any thought of a fugue. This aside, there were some nice ideas and good scoring which would have fitted very

[21] Jean François Lesueur (1760–1837), teacher of Berlioz, Gounod, and Ambroise Thomas.
[22] Charles Henri Plantade (1764–1839).

well into a comic opera. The final allegro, presumably to the words "*Dona nobis pacem*" (I cannot be sure, since the French pronounce Latin in a manner wholly unintelligible to the German ear) was so entirely in the style of an opera finale (including a tempo three or four times too fast) that when it was over, I quite forgot where I was and awaited the fall of the curtain and a burst of applause.

On December 24 we heard the so-called *messe de minuit*, this time a composition of Lesueur. First we had to undergo a formidable test of patience, listening for two hours, from ten o'clock until midnight, to nothing but psalms, sung in the most monotonous manner, and relieved from time to time with barbaric interludes by the organ. Finally, at midnight, the mass began. Again the same frivolous theater style as Plantade's, only even more repulsive at this solemn midnight hour.

What surprised me most, particularly with Lesueur, who enjoys the reputation of an excellent harmonist, and teaches harmony, if I am not mistaken, at the Paris Conservatory, was the want of even four-voiced writing. Two-voiced writing may have its place in the opera, the sopranos singing with the tenors and the altos with the basses. It eases the problem of the normally bad theater choruses, and it makes for a better concentration of available vocal resources. But I find it barbaric to extend this device to the church, and I am curious as to what Lesueur's intentions are. He is certainly a thoughtful artist.

In place of the Offertory there were variations by Nadermann[23] for harp, horn, and cello. You may remem-

[23] François Joseph Nadermann (c.1773–1835), son of a famous harp

ber that, in Germany, I found a serious symphonic movement too worldly for this situation, and you can easily imagine what a repulsive impression these "galant" French harp variations made upon me at a midnight mass. And yet, all around me were people praying. How can they entertain a pious thought to such trivial music? Either the music has no meaning for them, or they have the happy faculty of not hearing it at all! Otherwise, they could only be reminded of the ballet of the Grand Opera, where these three instruments are similarly employed for the most voluptuous dances. Although it was the favorite instrument of a pious kind in olden times, the harp should nevertheless be banned from the church, if only because it is utterly unsuited to the elevated style which alone is appropriate to religious music.

And now will you believe me when I tell you that even the worthy master, Cherubini, himself, has been seduced by this bad example and that the theater style is often predominant in his masses? He redeems himself in such passages, to be sure, by excellent, effective music. But who can enjoy it who cannot forget the place where he hears it? That Cherubini deserts the true church style would be less regrettable if there were not those numbers in which he shows what he can do with it. Many single movements in his masses, notably the wonderfully worked-out fugues and particularly his *Pater Noster* (except for the worldly close) provide the most eloquent evidence. However, once one has learned not to take offense at this often luxuriant style, he can find much artistic pleasure in it.

maker and himself considered one of the outstanding harp virtuosos of the time. He composed much chamber music for that instrument.

With the richness of his invention, his select, often exotic harmonies, and his clever exploitation of available resources, gained through long experience, Cherubini can achieve such overpowering effects that one is swept along, even against his will, and, rendered oblivious to the obviously contrived, surrenders to his feelings and his pleasure. What would this man not have accomplished if he had written for Germans instead of for Frenchmen!

Paris, January 30, 1821

I have now fulfilled another, hardly less important purpose of our visit here, namely, to hear the best of the local violinists. Baillot gave a musicale at his house at my request. I heard Lafont at his concert, and Habeneck and the younger Kreutzer at special matinees. If you ask me now which of the four I liked the best, I would say Lafont, if we are speaking solely of execution. His playing combines beauty of tone, the utmost purity, strength, and charm. He would be a perfect violinist if he could add deep feeling to these splendid virtues, and if he were not so hopelessly a victim of the habit, common to the French school, of accenting the last note of every phrase. Of feeling, without which one can neither compose nor play a good adagio, he seems to have none, which is more or less true of all the French players. Although he embellishes his slow movements with many elegant and tasteful ornaments, he leaves the listener cold. Generally speaking, adagios are regarded here as the least important movements, and are retained, apparently, only to separate the two fast movements and to contribute to their effectiveness by contrast.

The indifference, even insensibility, of the French to all that stimulates feeling probably explains why my adagios, and my way of playing them, have been less effective here than my brilliant allegros. Spoiled by the applause expended upon them previously by the Germans, Italians, Dutch, and English, I was rather hurt, at first, to find them so little admired by the French. Afterwards, however, having noted how seldom their own artists ever give them a serious adagio, and how little their taste for such things has been cultivated, I didn't feel as bad about it.

The accentuation of the last note of a phrase by increased pressure and a rapid upward sweep of the bow is common, more or less, to all the French violinists, and to none more conspicuously than Lafont. I cannot imagine how such a practice could have been generally adopted, for the effect is as if a speaker were to continually accent the short last syllables. If they had modeled the phrasing of their cantabiles on human song (which I believe every instrumentalist should do), they would never have strayed into such byways. The Parisians are by now so accustomed to this perversity that they find the playing of a stranger not similarly perverse much too simple.

That Lafont's virtuosity is limited to a few pieces, and that he practices a concerto for years before playing it in public, is well known. Since I have experienced the perfection of execution he achieves thereby, I hesitate to criticize such a restricted concentration of energy, but I could certainly not do it myself. I cannot understand how anyone can play the same thing from four to six hours every day, nor why such a mechanical procedure is not fatal to truly artistic feeling.

247

Baillot is, technically, almost Lafont's equal, and his versatility is proof that his technic has been achieved without recourse to such drastic measures. In addition to his own compositions he plays almost everything else, both old and new. He gave us that evening a quintet by Boccherini, a quartet by Haydn, and three pieces of his own: a concerto, an *air varié*, and a rondo. He played them all impeccably and with a type of expression apparently characteristic of him. I found it rather contrived than spontaneous. Indeed, his interpretive style in general, because of the emphasis upon means rather than ends, has a mannered effect. His bowing is skillful and rich in nuances, although not as free as Lafont's, and his tone, consequently less beautiful. The mechanism of up-bow and down-bow is all too audible. His compositions are distinguished from those of his Parisian colleagues by their correctness, nor can they be denied a certain originality. But there is something contrived, mannered, and old-fashioned about them which leaves the listener untouched.

As you know, he favors these quintets of Boccherini. I know about a dozen of them, and was curious to see whether he would play them in such a way as to make one oblivious to their superficiality. Although he played this one quintet beautifully, I was more unpleasantly affected than ever before by the childishness of the melodies and the thinness of the three-voiced harmonies. It is inconceivable to me how a cultivated artist such as Baillot, who is well acquainted with our treasures in this field, can bring himself to go on playing music which can only be supported with due regard for the time and circumstances under which it was written. That they are listened to here as eagerly and with as much pleasure as the music of Mozart only strengthens my conviction that the Parisians cannot distinguish between good and bad and that they are, furthermore, in their artistic cultivation, at least fifty years behind the times.

From Habeneck, I heard two *airs variés* of his own composition. He is a brilliant violinist, who can play a lot of notes with speed and facility. His tone and his bowing tend to be rough.

The younger Kreutzer, brother and pupil of the elder, played me a new, very brilliant and charming trio of his brother's. His playing reminded me of his brother, and convinced me that of all the Paris violinists, they are the most cultivated. The younger brother lacks physical strength, and often must give up playing for a month at a time. His tone is therefore a bit dull. Otherwise his playing is clean, spirited, and expressive.

Moscheles has been here the past four weeks. His extremely brilliant playing has created a sensation. He has won over both the laymen and the professionals, the former by his playing of his imaginative compositions, the latter primarily by his free improvisations, in which he succeeds in approaching the French taste, at least to the extent that his Germanism permits.

In a few days we shall return to Germany by way of Nancy and Strasbourg, and be able to greet you soon again in our beloved fatherland.

Until then, farewell!

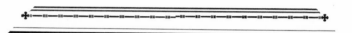

EPILOGUE

After leaving Paris, the Spohrs settled briefly in Dresden, where Weber was preparing the premiere of *Der Freischuetz*. During their stay, Weber was offered the post of musical director to the Elector of Hesse-Kassel. He was unwilling to leave Dresden, and proposed Spohr for the position. It was offered to Spohr as a lifetime appointment, and he entered upon his new duties on New Year's day, 1822.

Spohr held this post until his retirement in 1857. Dorette died in 1834. Two years later, he married Marianne Pfeiffer, a pianist. At Kassel, Spohr led the life of a celebrated virtuoso, composer, and conductor, but his days as a great traveler were over, discounting a number of trips to England where his oratorios, operas, symphonies, concertos, and chamber music enjoyed great popularity, and where he was much in demand as a conductor.

He made history at Kassel by his early sponsorship of

Wagner, producing *The Flying Dutchman* there in 1842, and *Tannhaeuser* in 1853. Although his account of his early career betrays little interest in politics, he was much concerned with the revolutionary developments of 1832 and 1848, siding with the radicals. This soured his relationship with the Elector and contributed to his early retirement. He died in Kassel, October 22, 1859.

INDEX

DATE DUE

#47-0108 Peel Off Pressure Sensitive